Holt French Level 3

Allez, viens! ®

Lesson Planner

HOLT, RINEHART AND WINSTON
Harcourt Brace & Company

Austin • New York • Orlando • Atlanta • San Francisco • Boston • Dallas • Toronto • London

Contributing Consultants, Reviewers, and Writers:

Jane Canales
Austin, TX

Bob Didsbury
Raleigh, NC

Joan Manley
El Paso, TX

Françoise Turner
El Paso, TX

Cover Photo Credit
Musée d'Orsay: Digital Stock Corp.

ALLEZ, VIENS! is a registered trademark licensed to Holt, Rinehart and Winston.

Printed in the United States of America

ISBN 0-03-054441-6

1 2 3 4 5 6 7   021   03 02 01 00 99

Table of Contents

To the Teacher

The *Lesson Planner* is designed to guide you through *Allez, viens!*, Level 3, suggesting a sequence of activities and material for each chapter to best suit your needs and those of your students. You will find that the *Lesson Planner* for *Allez, viens!*, Level 3 facilitates the planning, execution, and documentation of your classroom work.

Standards for Foreign Language Learning

At the end of each section of the lesson plan is a table showing the correlations of the *Pupil's Edition* and the *Annotated Teacher's Edition* to the Standards for Foreign Language Learning. In addition, the chart on page v provides a summary of the five major goals and the standards within each goal, so that you can more easily understand the correlation within each section of the *Lesson Planner*. For more information on the Standards for Foreign Language Learning, see the Robert LaBouve essay on pages T46 and T47 of the Level 3 *Allez, viens! Annotated Teacher's Edition*.

Homework Calendar Master

On page vi you will find a Homework Calendar Master that you can copy and distribute to your class so that you and your students can keep track of their assignments. The master is designed to contain homework assignments for one week.

Sample Lesson Plan for a Multi-Level Class

Many foreign language teachers are faced with the dilemma of having students of various levels mixed together in one class. This is most commonly seen with upper level students, when enrollments are too low to justify two separate classes, or when schedule conflicts prohibit students from enrolling in the appropriate class. The sample lesson plan on pages vii–x suggests one way you might organize a class consisting of both Level 3 and Level 4 students, using Chapter 4 of *Allez, viens!*, Level 3. For more information about this chapter, such as objectives, additional suggestions, resources, and correlations to the Standards for Foreign Language Learning, see the standard lesson plans for Chapter 4 on pages 17–21.

Sample Block Scheduling Lesson Plan

There are many different configurations for block scheduling and modified block scheduling. The sample lesson plan included in this *Lesson Planner* shows how to schedule Chapter 5 of *Allez, viens!*, Level 3, for a block program that has periods of 90 minutes held every other day, with the semester divided into three six-week periods. Allowing two weeks for interrupted class time due to schoolwide testing or other special events and final semester exams, six chapters of *Allez, viens!* can be covered in each of two 16-week semesters, including weekly assessment. This translates into seven or eight days per chapter. For objectives, additional suggestions, resources, and correlations to the Standards for Foreign Language Learning, see the lesson plan for each particular chapter.

Chapter-Specific Lesson Plans

Each chapter's lesson plan consists of objectives, suggestions for core instruction, recommendations beyond the core lesson for block scheduling, additional resources in the *Allez, viens!* program, and correlations to the Standards for Foreign Language Learning. Five pages of lesson plans, arranged by chapter section, are provided for each chapter. The first page gives suggestions for the Location Opener, Chapter Opener, and **Mise en train.** The second page's lesson plan addresses the **Première étape;** the third, the **Remise en train;** the fourth, the **Deuxième étape;** and the fifth, **Lisons!** and **Mise en pratique,** which includes suggestions for using **Que sais-je...?** and **Vocabulaire.**

Suggestions for block scheduling are found in shaded boxes, at point of use, throughout the lesson plan. Although they may require some extra setup time, the activities found in the shaded boxes allow students to deepen or extend their learning, or use their new learning in a different way. Teachers following a traditional schedule may wish to incorporate some of these suggestions, provided they have adequate time available.

Standards for Foreign Language Learning

COMMUNICATION **Communicate in Languages Other Than English**	**Standard 1.1:** Students engage in conversations, provide and obtain information, express feelings and emotions, and exchange opinions. **Standard 1.2:** Students understand and interpret written and spoken language on a variety of topics. **Standard 1.3:** Students present information, concepts, and ideas to an audience of listeners or readers on a variety of topics.
CULTURES **Gain Knowledge and Understanding of Other Cultures**	**Standard 2.1:** Students demonstrate an understanding of the relationship between the practices and perspectives of the culture studied. **Standard 2.2:** Students demonstrate an understanding of the relationship between the products and perspectives of the culture studied.
CONNECTIONS **Connect with Other Disciplines and Acquire Information**	**Standard 3.1:** Students reinforce and further their knowledge of other disciplines through the foreign language. **Standard 3.2:** Students acquire information and recognize the distinctive viewpoints that are only available through the foreign language and its cultures.
COMPARISONS **Develop Insight into the Nature of Language and Culture**	**Standard 4.1:** Students demonstrate understanding of the nature of language through comparisons of the language studied and their own. **Standard 4.2:** Students demonstrate understanding of the concept of culture through comparisons of the cultures studied and their own.
COMMUNITIES **Participate in Multilingual Communities at Home and Around the World**	**Standard 5.1:** Students use the language both within and beyond the school setting. **Standard 5.2:** Students show evidence of becoming life-long learners by using the language for personal enjoyment and enrichment.

National Standards in Foreign Langauge Education Project: "National Standards Report" from *Standards for Foreign Language Learning: Preparing for the 21st Century.* Copyright © 1996 by National Standards in Foreign Language Education Project.

Devoirs à rendre

Dates : du **lundi** _____ au **vendredi** _____

Jour	Devoirs
lundi le ⬜ _____ _____ _____	_Textbook:_ _____ _P & A:_ _____ _G & V:_ _____ _CD-ROM:_ _____ _Other:_ _____
mardi le ⬜ _____ _____ _____	_Textbook:_ _____ _P & A:_ _____ _G & V:_ _____ _CD-ROM:_ _____ _Other:_ _____
mercredi le ⬜ _____ _____ _____	_Textbook:_ _____ _P & A:_ _____ _G & V:_ _____ _CD-ROM:_ _____ _Other:_ _____
jeudi le ⬜ _____ _____ _____	_Textbook:_ _____ _P & A:_ _____ _G & V:_ _____ _CD-ROM:_ _____ _Other:_ _____
vendredi le ⬜ _____ _____ _____	_Textbook:_ _____ _P & A:_ _____ _G & V:_ _____ _CD-ROM:_ _____ _Other:_ _____

Allez, viens! Level 3

Sample Lesson Plan for a Multi-Level Class

In a multi-level classroom environment, it is important to relieve any anxiety students might have about being placed in a multi-level learning situation. Students should be reassured that it is not demeaning or a waste of time to recycle activities or to share knowledge and skills with fellow students. Third-year students need to know that they are not second-class citizens and that they can benefit from their classmates' greater experience with the language. Fourth-year students need reassurance that you will devote time to them and challenge them with different assignments. Fourth-year students should also be made aware of the benefits they will gain by helping or teaching third-year students, including increased confidence in their own language skills and the satisfaction of helping others achieve.

You can relieve your own apprehension by remembering that, after one year of classroom instruction, no class is ever truly homogeneous. Despite being made up of students with the same amount of "seat time," every class comprises multiple layers of language skills, knowledge, motivation, and ability.

Addressing these individual differences in a single-level classroom requires effort and good planning, and you will find the same to be true of a multi-level classroom. Meeting the needs of students at different levels will be made easier if you work towards the goal of making students less dependent on you for the successful completion of their activities, placing more responsibility for learning on the students, and by implementing creative individual, pair, and group activities.

Pair and group activities are very effective in multi-level classrooms and can accomplish a variety of objectives, depending on how you group your students. For example, pairing a fourth-year student with a third-year student would create a peer-tutoring situation, and grouping several fourth and third-year students together could foster a cross-level attitude of cooperation and teamwork. There will be other times when you will want to group students by level, for example, when providing students with material that is appropriate for their level, but which would be either too basic or too advanced for students at a different level. The decision to group students in pairs or groups, multi-level or same level, should be tied to your goals for that day. You may find it effective to have the students take part in the decision as to what type of group works best for them.

Chapter 4

BEGINNING THE CHAPTER (pp. 80–84)

(All references in this lesson plan are taken from *Allez, viens!,* Level 3.)

OBJECTIVES
To get acquainted with the functional expressions, grammar, and vocabulary that will be covered in this chapter.

BOTH LEVELS TOGETHER
- Use the Focusing on Outcomes, p. 81, to introduce students to what they will be learning in this chapter.
- As per Motivating Activity, p. 80, have students in mixed-level groups work to create a list of the "looks" that are currently popular. Ask students to look through fashion magazines for photographs of clothing that they think is "in."

MISE EN TRAIN (pp. 82–84)

LEVEL 3 STUDENTS
Divide Level 3 students into groups of three and have them do the Motivating Activity on page 82. You might want to have each of the groups exchange pictures and write captions for the pictures they receive.

LEVEL 4 STUDENTS
- Using the information in the Culture Notes on page 80 as a starting point, have groups of students prepare a detailed description of the six photographs on pages 82–83. You might have them describe the clothing and assign names, ages, nationalities, and other background information to the models. This will give students the opportunity to recycle previously used vocabulary and expressions.

BOTH LEVELS TOGETHER
- Have each group select representatives to report their results to the rest of the class. (The Level 3 group can report the captions they came up with; the Level 4 group can introduce the rest of the class to the six personalities they created.)
- Place students in groups of three, with one Level 4 students in each group if possible. Assign each group a section of the **Mise en train** and have one student direct the other two as they rehearse and present their section of the dialogue between Jérôme and Axcelle.

LEVEL 3 STUDENTS
- Have students do Activities 1–3, p. 84, orally, as a group.

LEVEL 4 STUDENTS
- Have students do Activity 6, p. 84, in writing.

BOTH LEVELS TOGETHER

- Have students share what they know about French fashion, style shows, etc. See Culture Note, p. 83 and the **Note Culturelle**, p. 84, for additional information. If French catalogues are available, use them as a basis for information and discussion. If not, use American catalogues.

PREMIERE ETAPE (pp. 85–91)

OBJECTIVES

Students will learn to ask for and give opinions, ask which one(s), and point out and identify people and things.

BOTH LEVELS TOGETHER

- Do Motivate, p. 85.

LEVEL 4 STUDENTS

- Have students write detailed descriptions of three or four different outfits.

LEVEL 3 STUDENTS

- Do Presentation: **Vocabulaire**, p. 85.

BOTH LEVELS TOGETHER

- Have Level 4 students read their descriptions aloud, as Level 3 students offer opinions about where one might where such an outfit.
  - **Une longue robe bleu, des haut talons, des boucles d'oreille, une montre et un pendentif.**
  - **On peut le porter à l'église.**
- Play the audio recording for Activity 7, p. 85 (Audio CD 4) and ask members of the class to provide the answers.

LEVEL 3 STUDENTS

- Have students do Activities 1 and 4, *Grammar and Vocabulary Workbook,* pp. 29-30.

LEVEL 4 STUDENTS

- Go over **Vocabulaire à la carte**, p. 86, with Level 4 students. Then have students write a description of an outfit, incorporating at least two or three of the words from **Vocabulaire à la carte.**

BOTH LEVELS TOGETHER

- Have Level 4 students use their drawings to present the vocabulary from **Vocabulaire à la carte** to the Level 3 students.
- Have students do Activity 9, p. 86. Ask Level 4 students to include words from **Vocabulaire à la carte** in their sentences.
- Review object pronouns with all students. See **Reteaching**, p. 86.
- Present **Comment dit-on... ?**, p. 86. Have students do Activity 10, p. 86 and check for comprehension.
- Have students do Activity 11, p. 87. Encourage Level 4 students to make their conversations four to five lines long. Have Level 4 students read their conversations out loud, and ask Level 3 students to identify whether each one expresses a favorable or unfavorable opinion.
- Present the **Vocabulaire**, p. 87, using magazine photographs and illustrations. Hold up additional examples, and have students suggest an appropriate adjective.

LEVEL 3 STUDENTS

- Have Level 3 students do Activities 8 and 10, *Grammar and Vocabulary Workbook,* pp. 32–33.
- Have students do Activity 13, p. 87.

LEVEL 4 STUDENTS

- Have students do Activity 12, p. 87, and then set up each situation as a short skit.

BOTH LEVELS TOGETHER

- Have Level 4 students perform Activity 12 for the Level 3 students, and then ask comprehension questions about each skit.
- Have students work in groups of four, with two Level 3 students and two Level 4 students in each group, to do Activity 15, p. 88. First, have them brainstorm their ideas as a group. Then have the Level 3 students design the outfits for their fashion line (15a) and have the Level 4 students prepare and write the advertising slogans (15b). Have the groups make their presentations to the rest of the class and get feedback from the audience.
- Do Presentation: **Comment dit-on... ?**, p. 88, and then play the audio recording for Activity 6 (Audio CD 4).
- Do Presentation: **Grammaire**, p. 89. Play the recording for Activity 17, p. 89 and check for comprehension.

LEVEL 3 STUDENTS

- Have students do Activity 18 and Additional Practice, p. 89.

LEVEL 4 STUDENTS

- Have students work in pairs to create conversations about fashion, using *Teaching Transparency 4–1.* See **Suggestions for Using Teaching Transparency 4–1**, Suggestion 4.

BOTH LEVELS TOGETHER

- Have volunteers from both levels present their conversations to the whole group.
- Have students take Quiz 4-1A, *Testing Program,* pp. 66–67.
- Have students watch the video for **Panorama Culturel**, *Video Program* (Videocassette 2).

LEVEL 3 STUDENTS

- Have students discuss the questions in **Qu'en penses-tu?** and **Questions**, p. 91.

LEVEL 4 STUDENTS

- Have students do the second Post-viewing activity for the **Panorama Culturel**, *Video Guide,* p. 23. Divide students into two groups, and have each group brainstorm phrases and words they might need to debate the questions.

BOTH LEVELS TOGETHER

- Have Level 4 students debate the questions in the second Post-viewing activity for the **Panorama Culturel**, *Video Guide,* p. 23, with the Level 3 students as their audience. Ask Level 3 students to work in pairs to come up with two or three questions to ask after the debate.

LEVEL 3 STUDENTS

- Have students take Quiz 4-1B, *Testing Program,* pp. 68–70.

- Have students do Situation 4-1: Role-play, *Activities for Communication,* p. 86.

LEVEL 4 STUDENTS
- Have students work in pairs to prepare and present the Performance Assessment, *Annotated Teacher's Edition,* p. 90.

REMISE EN TRAIN (pp. 92–93)

BOTH LEVELS TOGETHER
After doing Motivating Activity, p. 92, have students create their own illustrations or find magazine pictures of different hairstyles and display them in the classroom.

LEVEL 3 STUDENTS
- Do Presentation, p. 92, and have students complete Activities 21–23.

LEVEL 4 STUDENTS
- Have students work in pairs to create their own conversation between two friends who are at a hair salon, using the **Remise en train** as a model. One of them wants to get a "new look" and discusses possible hairstyles based on what different customers at the salon are having done. The partner should comment on the different hairstyles and give advice on what would be the best choice. Then have the Level 4 students present their conversations to the Level 3 students.

LEVEL 3 STUDENTS
- Have students discuss their reactions to Perrine's hairstyle.
- Ask them to discuss together what they would do and say to a friend who got an unusual, even unattractive, hairstyle and asked them their opinion.

LEVEL 4 STUDENTS
- Have students do Activity 25, p. 93 in writing.

BOTH LEVELS TOGETHER
- Divide the class into groups with at least one Level 4 student in each group. Have students use the information in the **Note Culturelle,** p. 93 to research styles that are more American or French. Have them use illustrations or pictures to discuss with the other groups the differences they found.

DEUXIEME ETAPE (pp. 94–97)

OBJECTIVES
To pay and respond to compliments and reassure someone.

BOTH LEVELS TOGETHER
- Do Motivate, p. 94.

LEVEL 4 STUDENTS
- Have students look at the **Vocabulaire** picture on page 94 and imagine and write as many statements as possible, describing what the people in the picture might say to one another.

LEVEL 3 STUDENTS
- Do Presentation: **Vocabulaire,** p. 94.

BOTH LEVELS TOGETHER
- Have the Level 4 students read the statements they prepared to the Level 3 students, who can then

guess to which persons the statements refer.
- Have students work in pairs to complete Activity 27, p. 94.
- Do Presentation: **Grammaire,** p. 95.
- Have students do Activities 28 and 29, p. 95. See Additional Practice, p. 95.
- Present **A la française,** p. 95 and have students practice the pronunciation of each phrase.
- Have students work in mixed-level pairs to do the Teaching Suggestion, p. 95. Have volunteers perform their conversations in front of the class.
- Have students take Quiz 4-2A, *Testing Program,* pp. 71–72 and go over it in small, mixed-level groups.

LEVEL 3 STUDENTS
- Have students do Activities 22 and 23, *Grammar and Vocabulary Workbook,* p. 40.

LEVEL 4 STUDENTS
- Show *Teaching Transparency 4-2* and have students write a journal entry based on the images at the top of the transparency. See **Suggestions for Using Teaching Transparency 4-2,** Suggestion 4.

BOTH LEVELS TOGETHER
- Have students complete Activity 30, p. 96. See Building On Previous Skills, p. 96.
- Do Presentation: **Comment dit-on...?,** p. 96.
- Play the audio recording for Activity 31, p. 96 (Audio CD 4). Ask the Level 3 students to note if the people are responding to a compliment or reassuring someone. Have the Level 4 students jot down the functional expressions they hear in each conversation. Check the answers orally.
- Have students work in pairs to do Activities 32 and 33, p. 97.

LEVEL 3 STUDENTS
- Have students take Quiz 4-2B, *Testing Program,* pp. 73–74.
- Have students do Situation 4-2: Role-Play, *Activities for Communication,* p. 96.

LEVEL 4 STUDENTS
- Have students work in pairs to prepare and present Performance Assessment, *Annotated Teacher's Edition* p. 97.

LISONS! (pp. 98–100)

OBJECTIVES
- Students will learn to build on what they know.

BOTH LEVELS TOGETHER
- Do Motivating Activity, and read and discuss **De bons conseils,** p. 98.

LEVEL 4 STUDENTS
- Have students look through French fashion magazines and select one short article (½ page–1 page) or section of an article about fashion that interests them. Have them read the article for general understanding. They should then write a list and provide definitions for eight to ten vocabulary terms readers might want to know. They should also create and provide the answers for five general comprehension questions about the reading and a quiz of ten short answer questions about the reading.

LEVEL 3 STUDENTS
- Have students work in small groups to read pages 98–99 and do Activities A–H.
- Read and discuss Activities I–N, p. 100, as a class.

ECRIVONS! (p. 101)

OBJECTIVES
Students will learn to generate ideas by asking questions.

BOTH LEVELS TOGETHER
- Read and discuss **De bons conseils,** p. 101.
- Have students do Prewriting: Motivating Activity and Activities A–C, p. 101.
- See also Postwriting: Teaching Suggestions, p. 101.

MISE EN PRATIQUE (pp. 102–105)

OBJECTIVES
Students will review and integrate all four skills and cultural information in preparation for Chapter 4 assessment.

BOTH LEVELS TOGETHER
- Have the students play the game **J'en doute** on page 90, which will help all the students practice using the vocabulary in context.
- Have students do Activities 1–5, pp. 102–103.
- As homework, have students try to do the **Que sais-je?** activities on page 104.

QUE SAIS-JE? (pp. 104–105)

OBJECTIVES
Students will evaluate their understanding of the functions, vocabulary, grammar, and culture presented in Chapter 4.

BOTH LEVELS TOGETHER
- Have students do **Que sais-je?** Activities 1–8, p. 104 orally.
- Divide the class into small groups, with at least one Level 4 student in each group. See the Group Work suggestion on page 104 to practice all the material learned in this chapter.

ASSESSMENT

LEVEL 3 STUDENTS
- Have students take Chapter Test, *Testing Program,* pp. 75–80.

LEVEL 4 STUDENTS
- While the Level 3 students are taking the test, have the Level 4 students do **Mon journal,** *Practice and Activity Book,* p. 148. Make sure you and the students together have established a rubric for such a writing assignment, so that students know how much attention they have to pay to detail, how much each part will be counted, etc.

BOTH LEVELS TOGETHER
- Have students work in mixed-level groups to do Project: **Un Magazine de mode,** p. 79I.

Sample High School Lesson Plan for Block Scheduling

There are many different configurations for block scheduling and modified block scheduling. Block periods may last for 65, 80, 90, 100, 118, or 140 minutes. A course may be scheduled for every day, every other day, or two days a week. Some schools schedule a year's work in one semester (4 subjects per semester, four classes of 90 minutes daily) while others spread the curriculum over two semesters. The following sample lesson plan shows how to schedule Chapter 5 of *Allez, viens!*, Level 3, for a block program that has periods of 90 minutes held every other day, with the semester divided into three six-week periods. Allowing two weeks for interruptions to class time due to school-wide testing or other special events and a final semester exam, six chapters of *Allez, viens!*, Level 3, are covered in each of two 16-week semesters (including weekly assessment). This translates into seven to eight days per chapter. For objectives, additional suggestions, resources, and correlations to the Standards for Foreign Language Learning, see the standard lesson plans for Chapter 5 on pages 22–26.

Chapitre 5   C'est notre avenir

DAY ONE

LOCATION OPENER (pp. 106–109)
Objectives: Students will identify countries that make up French-speaking Africa and learn about their culture.

- See Motivating Activity, p. 106. You may wish to use *Map Transparency 4:* **L'Afrique francophone** in your discussion.
- See Using the Map and Terms in the Almanac, p. 107.
- Divide students into seven groups, assigning each group a picture from pages 108–109. Have students choose a representative for their group. Have students discuss the content of their captions and tell where in **L'Afrique francophone** they may find the subject of their photos. You may want to share the additional information from Using the Photo Essay on page 108 with the selected groups.
- Have the students choose a representative from their group to present their findings to the rest of the groups.
- Play **Vidéoclip 4**, Chapter 5 of the *Video Program* (Videocassette 2). Discuss the footage of Senegal with students. You might have students do the corresponding activity, *Video Guide,* p. 34.

CHAPTER OPENER (pp. 110–111)
Objectives: Students will identify the learning outcomes in Chapter 5.

- See Motivating Activity, p. 110 and Culture Notes, pp. 110-111.
- Read and discuss the chapter outcomes, p. 111. See Focusing on Outcomes, p. 111.

MISE EN TRAIN (pp. 112–114)
Objectives: Students will learn about the future plans of six teenagers from Senegal.

- See Motivating Activity, p. 112.
- Do Presentation: **L'avenir, c'est demain,** p. 112 (Audio CD 5). See Language Note, p. 112.
- Divide the class into six groups and do the activity suggested in Group Work, p. 113.
- Have students complete Activities 1–4, p. 114. Check answers as a class.
- Discuss **Note Culturelle,** p. 114. See Culture Note, p. 114.

HOMEWORK

- Activity 5, p. 114. Students may wish to record their responses in their journals.
- Activities 1 and 2, *Practice and Activity Book,* p. 49

DAY TWO

MISE EN TRAIN (pp. 112–114)

- Go over homework from Day 1: Activities 1 and 2, *Practice and Activity Book,* p. 49.

RENCONTRE CULTURELLE (p. 115)
Objectives: Students will describe and identify various aspects of the country of Senegal.

- Do Motivating Activity, p. 115, using *Map Transparency 4:* **L'Afrique francophone.**
- Have students read the picture captions in pairs. Ask students what their impressions of Senegal are, based on the photos.
- Read and discuss **Qu'en penses-tu?** and **Savais-tu que... ?,** p. 115 as a class.

- See Thinking Critically, p. 115. If students do a photo project for this activity, you might have them present their work in a photography exhibition and invite any French-speaking members of your community to attend.

PREMIERE ETAPE (pp. 116–119)
Objectives: Students will ask about and express intentions. They will also express conditions and possibilities.

- Have students recall the future plans of two of the Senegalese students they read about in **Mise en train.**
- Discuss Culture Note, p. 117.
- Do Presentation: **Vocabulaire,** p. 116. When students copy the expressions onto slips of paper, have them use the infinitive form.
- Have students complete Activity 6, p. 116 (Audio CD 5).
- Complete Additional Listening Activity 5-1, *Listening Activities,* p. 39.
- Make four columns on the board: *asking about intentions, expressing intentions, expressing conditions,* and *expressing possibilities.* Model the functional expressions from page 117, asking students to guess the category to which each expression belongs. You might have students refer to the **Mise en train,** pp. 112–113, to see if they can find any of the new expressions in the students' letters.
- Have students write Activity 4, *Practice and Activity Book,* p. 50.
- Have students do Activity 7, p. 117 (Audio CD 5) and check for comprehension.

HOMEWORK
- Activities 2 and 3, *Grammar and Vocabulary Worksheets,* pp. 41, 42

DAY THREE
PREMIERE ETAPE (pp. 116–119)
- Go over homework from Day 2: Activities 2 and 3, *Grammar and Vocabulary Worksheets,* pp. 41, 42
- Discuss **Tu te rappelles?,** p. 117. See Language Note, p. 117.
- Complete Reteaching suggestion on the subjunctive, p. 117.
- Complete Activity 8, p. 117, orally.
- Do Presentation: **Grammaire,** p. 118. See Language Note, p. 118.

- On a transparency, make a list of verbs, with some forms in the present tense and some in the future tense. Have students identify which forms are in the future tense and have them explain how they could tell the difference.
- Do Activities 9 and 10, p. 118–119, orally as a class.
- Have students write Activities 10 and 11, *Practice and Activity Book,* p. 53.
- Show *Transparency 5-1* and have students work in groups of three. Have them imagine and create the conversation that is taking place in the transparency scene. For additional suggestions see **Suggestions for Using Teaching Transparencies 5-1.**
- Review for quiz with Game: **Après le lycée...,** p. 119.

HOMEWORK
- Activity 12, p. 119
- Activities 10–12, *Grammar and Vocabulary Worksheets,* pp. 46–47
- Take Quiz 5-1A, *Testing Program,* pp. 89–90.
- Study for Quiz 5-1B *(Testing Program, pp. 91–92).*

DAY FOUR
PREMIERE ETAPE (pp. 116–119)
- Go over homework from Day 3: Activities 10–12, *Grammar and Vocabulary Worksheets,* pp. 46–47 and Quiz 5-1A.
- Have students take Quiz 5-1B.

REMISE EN TRAIN (pp. 120–121)
Objectives: Students will learn about a student's future plans after high school.
- Have students reread Omar's letter from **Mise en train,** p. 112. See Motivating Activity, p. 120.
- Do Presentation: **Remise en train,** p. 120 (Audio CD 5).
- Complete Activity 15, p. 120, as a class.
- Have students open their books to p. 121 or make a copy or transparency of Omar's letter. Have students identify to whom the letter is addressed and what information Omar is seeking.
- Have students work with a partner to complete Activities 16 and 17, p. 121.

PANORAMA CULTUREL (p. 122)

Objectives: Students will listen to and read about the professions some francophone teenagers want to pursue in the future.

- Discuss information found in Pre-viewing suggestions, *Video Guide,* p. 30.
- See Presentation, Video Guide, p. 122 and play the video for **Panorama Culturel,** Video Program (Videocassette 2). Before students answer the Questions on page 122, have them watch the video and complete the Panorama Culturel section on Activity Master 1, Video Guide, p. 33.
- Ask students to which interviewee they most relate. See Teaching Suggestion, p. 122.
- Complete the Post-viewing suggestions, *Video Guide,* p. 31.

DEUXIEME ETAPE (pp. 123–127)

Objectives: Students will ask about future plans, express wishes and indecision, give advice, request information, and write a formal letter.

- Have students refer back to the **Mise en train** on pages 112–113. Have them identify in English the professions that these teenagers want to pursue. Then have students scan the letters for what they they think are names of professions. List these professions on the board and ask students if they are interested in these professions.
- Do Presentation: **Vocabulaire,** p. 123.
- Call out a profession and ask a student or pairs of students to model the selected profession. Students can mime or use any available props to act out what a person in this profession would do. Then have students choose a profession, model it, and have their classmates identify the profession.
- Discuss **Note Culturelle,** p. 123.
- Complete Activity 18, p. 123 (Audio CD 5).
- Have students write Activities 14 and 17, *Grammar and Vocabulary Worksheets,* pp. 49–50.
- Introduce **Vocabulaire à la carte,** p. 124.
- Have students work in groups to complete Activity 22, p. 125 (Audio CD 5).

HOMEWORK

- Have students write Activity 23, p. 125, in their journals.

DAY FIVE

DEUXIEME ETAPE (pp. 123–127)

- Review professions by having students do Communicative Activity 5-2, *Activities for Communication,* pp. 19–20 with a partner.
- Do Presentation: **Comment dit-on... ?,** p. 124.
- See For Individual Needs: Tactile Learners, p. 124.
- Have students complete Activity 24, p. 126 (Audio CD 5).
- See Additional Practice, p. 124.
- Have students work in pairs to do Activity 25, p. 126.
- Do Presentation: **Grammaire,** p. 125
- Discuss Language Note, p. 125.
- Have students do Activity 18, *Practice and Activity Book,* p. 57
- Do Game: **Qu'est-ce que tu ferais?,** p. 109J.
- See Motivating Activity, p. 126.
- Have students look at Omar's letter on p. 121. Have them identify expressions they might use in beginning and ending a formal letter and asking for information. Then write each expression on a note card or sheet of paper and have students identify where in a formal letter they would find the expression.
- Complete Activity 28, p. 127 (Audio CD 5).
- Have students do Activity 21, *Grammar and Vocabulary Worksheets,* p. 53. Check answers as a class.
- Have students take Quiz 5-2A, *Testing Program,* pp. 93–94 and go over it as a class.

HOMEWORK

- Study for Quiz 5-2B, *Testing Program,* pp. 96–96.

DAY SIX

DEUXIEME ETAPE (pp. 123–127)

- Have students complete Situation Card 5-2: Interview and Role-play, *Activities for Communication,* pp. 19-20 with a partner.
- Do Game: **Catégories,** p. 127.
- Quiz 5-2B

LISONS (pp. 128–130)

Objectives: Students will read a passage from a novel.

- See Motivating Activity, p. 128.
- Read and discuss **De bons conseils,** p. 128.
- Complete Activity A, p. 129, orally with students.
- Discuss Teacher Note, p. 129.
- Have students complete Activities B–G, pp. 129-130.
- See Geography Link, p. 130.
- Complete Activities H–L, p. 130.

ECRIVONS (p. 131)
Objective: Students will write a formal letter to apply for a job listed in a classified ad.

- Discuss the writing strategy presented in **De bons conseils,** p. 131. Have students think of additional contexts in which this strategy would be useful.
- Have students complete the **Préparation** Activity A. See Teaching Suggestion to accompany Item 3 in Activity A, p. 131.
- Have students complete Activity B, p. 131. Before students begin, you may want to have them review the expressions for beginning and ending a formal letter on page 126.

HOMEWORK
- Activity 22, *Practice and Activity Book,* p. 59

DAY SEVEN
ECRIVONS (p. 131)
- Using the drafts they created in Activity B, have students complete Activity C, p. 131. See Teaching Suggestion to accompany Activity C, p. 131.

MISE EN PRATIQUE (pp. 132-133)
Objective: Students will review the functions, vocabulary, culture, and grammar in preparation for the Chapter Test.

- Complete Activity 1, p. 132. Have students correct the false statements in the activity to make them true.
- Have students complete Activity 2, p. 132, with a partner. See Building on Previous Skills, p. 132.
- Complete Activity 3, p. 132 (Audio CD 5). See Teaching Suggestion, p. 132.
- Have students complete Activity 5, p. 133 in pairs.

QUE SAIS-JE? (p. 134)
Objectives: Students will check their understanding of the functions, vocabulary, grammar, and culture presented in Chapter 5.

- Activities 1-5, *Pupil's Edition,* pp. 132; have students exchange papers with a partner to check answers.
- Have students write Activities 6-10, p. 134.
- Go over the **Que sais-je?** activities, p. 134 in class.

HOMEWORK
- Study for Chapter Test, *Testing Program,* pp. 97-102.

DAY EIGHT
- Help students review for the Chapter Test by playing the game **Dis-moi!** or doing the circumlocution activity, p. 135.

CHAPTER TEST
- Have students take the Chapter Test.
- Speaking Test, *Testing Program,* p. 297

Chapter Lesson Plans

CHAPITRE 1

France, les régions

Beginning the Chapter (p. T68–p. 8)

Activities in the shaded boxes enhance the basic lesson and are ideal for **block scheduling**.

 Lesson Plans

Location Opener

Objectives

Students will learn about famous people, historical events, and places in francophone Europe.

- See the first two pre-viewing suggestions, *Video Guide,* p. 1.
- Motivating Activity, Background Information, and History Link, p. T68
- Distribute copies of the *Map Transparency 1* copy master and a list of countries and cities. Have students write in the country and city names on their maps.
- Have students watch *Allez, viens en Europe francophone!, Video Program* (Videocassette 1).
- Viewing suggestions, *Video Guide,* p. 1
- Multicultural Link, p. 2, Using the Photo Essay and Culture Notes, pp. 2–3
- Post-viewing suggestions, *Video Guide,* p. 1

Chapter Opener

- Motivating Activity, p. 4
- Photo Flash!, pp. 4–5
- Focusing on Outcomes and Teaching Suggestion, p. 5

Mise en train

Objectives

Students will listen to a conversation between five friends who are reunited after their summer vacation.

- Motivating Activity, p. 6
- Presentation: **Les Retrouvailles,** p. 6 (Audio CD 1)
- See the first two Teaching Suggestions, p. 7. See also Language Note and Culture Notes, p. 7.
- Geography Link, p. 7
- Activities 1–5, p. 8. See the related Teaching Suggestions, p. 8.
- Activity 6, p. 8. See Building on Previous Skills, p. 8.
- Have students work in pairs and use the expressions from Activity 6 on page 8 to create short conversations about their own summer vacations.
- Have students do Activity 7, p. 8, in writing. Then have students discuss their answers in small groups.
- Activity 1, *Practice and Activity Book,* p. 1
- You may wish to show **Camille et compagnie,** *Premier Épisode : Les Retrouvailles* (Videocassette 1) as an alternative or in addition to the **Mise en train,** or you may show the video episode at the end of the chapter to review new material. **Camille et compagnie** is also available with French captions on *Videocassette 5.*
- Viewing suggestions and Post-viewing Activities, *Video Guide,* pp. 4–6

Resources

For correlated print and audio-visual materials, see *Annotated Teacher's Edition,* pp. 3A–3B.

STANDARDS FOR FOREIGN LANGUAGE LEARNING

Location Opener *Pupil's Edition:* (1.2; 3.2) *Annotated Teacher's Edition:* (2.2; 3.2; 4.2; 4.3)
Chapter Opener *Pupil's Edition:* (1.2) *Annotated Teacher's Edition:* (1.2; 2.2; 3.1; 3.2; 4.1; 5.2)
Mise en train *Pupil's Edition:* (1.2; 1.3) *Annotated Teacher's Edition:* (1.1; 1.2; 2.1; 2.2; 3.1; 4.1; 4.2; 4.3)

Allez, viens! Level 3

France, les régions

Première étape (pp. 9–13)

Activities in the shaded boxes enhance the basic lesson and are ideal for **block scheduling**.

Lesson Plans

Objectives
Students will learn to renew old acquaintances, inquire, express enthusiasm and dissatisfaction, exchange information, and ask and describe what a place was like.

Motivate
Jump Start! and/or Motivate, p. 9

Teach
1. Do the first Presentation: **Comment dit-on... ?,** p. 9.
2. Play the audio recording for Activity 8, p. 9 (Audio CD 1) and check for comprehension.
3. Activity 9, p. 9
4. Do the second Presentation: **Comment dit-on... ?,** p. 9.
5. Play the audio recording for Activity 10, p. 10 and check for comprehension.
6. Activities 3 and 4, *Practice and Activity Book,* pp. 3–4
7. Activity 11, p. 10. See For Individual Needs: Auditory Learners, p. 10.
8. Presentation: **Comment dit-on... ?,** p. 10
9. Activity 12, p. 10
   Game: **Memoire,** p. 10
10. Presentation: **Grammaire,** p. 11. See Reteaching: Reflexive Verbs, p. 11.
11. Play the audio recording for Activity 13, p. 11 and check for comprehension.
12. Activities 3 and 4, *Grammar and Vocabulary Workbook,* p. 3
13. Activity 14, p. 12
14. Game 2, Chapter 1, *Interactive CD-ROM Program* (Disc 1)
15. Presentation: **Comment dit-on... ?,** p. 12
16. Play the audio recording for Activity 15, p. 12 and check for comprehension.
17. Presentation: **Grammaire,** p. 13
    Activities 16–19, p. 13

Additional Practice Options for Première étape
- *Grammar and Vocabulary Workbook,* pp. 1–5
- *Practice and Activity Book,* pp. 2–5
- Communicative Activities 1-1A and 1-1B, *Activities for Communication,* pp. 1–2
- Situation 1-1: Interview and Role-play, *Activities for Communication,* pp. 89–90
- Realia 1-1, *Activities for Communication,* pp. 51, 53
- Additional Listening Activities 1-1, 1-2 and 1-3, *Listening Activities,* pp. 7–8 (Audio CD 1)
- *Interactive CD-ROM Program* (Disc 1)
- *Teaching Transparency 1-1, Teaching Transparencies*
- Additional Grammar Practice, *Pupil's Edition,* Activities 1–5, pp. R53–R54
- **Vidéoclip 1,** *Video Program* (Videocassette 1). See *Video Guide,* pp. 5 and 7–8 for suggestions and activities.

Close
Close, p. 13

Assess
Quiz 1-1A, Quiz 1-1B, *Testing Program,* pp. 1–4, and/or Performance Assessment, *Annotated Teacher's Edition,* p. 13

STANDARDS FOR FOREIGN LANGUAGE LEARNING
Première étape *Pupil's Edition:* (1.1; 1.2; 1.3; 5.1; 5;2) *Annotated Teacher's Edition:* (1.1; 1.2; 1.3)

France, les régions

Remise en train (pp. 14–16)

Activities in the shaded boxes enhance the basic lesson and are ideal for **block scheduling**.

Lesson Plans

Objectives
Students will listen as some teenagers order a meal at an Alsatian restaurant.

- Presentation: **Bon appétit!**, p. 14 (Audio CD 1)
- Teaching Suggestions and Thinking Critically: Comparing and Contrasting, p. 14
- Culture Notes and Language Note, p. 15
- Activities 20–23, pp. 14–15
- Play the audio recording for Activity 24, p. 15 and check for comprehension. See the related Teaching Suggestion and Teacher Note, p. 15.
- Have students work in pairs to do Activity 25, p. 15.
- Additional Practice, p. 15
- Have students work in small groups to do Math Link, p. 15.
- Have students imagine they are in a restaurant. Ask them to work in small groups and use the expressions from Activity 23, p. 15, to create a conversation.
- Activity 10, *Practice and Activity Book*, p. 6
- As an alternative or in addition to the **Remise en train,** you may wish to show *Camille et compagnie, Premier Épisode : Les Retrouvailles* on Videocassette 1 again. For suggestions and activities, see the *Video Guide*, pp. 4 and 6.
- Motivating Activity, p. 16
- Pre-viewing suggestions for **Panorama Culturel**, *Video Guide*, p. 5
- Pre-viewing Activity 4, *Video Guide*, p. 7
- Do Presentation: **Panorama Culturel**, p. 16, using *Video Program* (Videocassette 1).
- Viewing Activity 5, *Video Guide*, p. 7
- Read and discuss the questions in **Qu'en penses-tu?**, p. 16.
- Activities 19–21, *Practice and Activity Book*, p. 12
- Post-viewing suggestion, *Video Guide*, p. 5
- Pre-viewing suggestion for **Vidéoclip 1**, *Video Guide*, p. 5
- Have students watch **Vidéoclip 1**, *Video Program* (Videocassette 1).
- Viewing and Post-viewing Activities, *Video Guide*, pp. 7–8
- Post-viewing suggestions, *Video Guide*, p. 5
- Multicultural Link, p. 16

STANDARDS FOR FOREIGN LANGUAGE LEARNING
Remise en train   *Pupil's Edition:* (1.2; 1.3; 2.2; 3.1) *Annotated Teacher's Edition:* (1.2; 1.3; 2.1; 2.2; 3.1; 3.2; 4.2)

France, les régions

Deuxième étape (pp. 17–19)

Activities in the shaded boxes enhance the basic lesson and are ideal for **block scheduling**.

Lesson Plans

Objectives

Students will learn to express indecision, make recommendations, order, and ask for details.

Motivate

Jump Start! and/or Motivate, p. 17

Teach

1. Presentation: **Comment dit-on… ?,** p. 17
2. Play the audio recording for Activity 26, p. 17 and check for comprehension.
3. Presentation: **Vocabulaire,** p. 17. See Building on Previous Skills, p. 17.
   Have students listen to Activity 26 again and note the foods that are being considered or recommended.
4. Activity 27, p. 18
5. Play the audio recording for Activity 28, p. 18 and check for comprehension. See For Individual Needs: Slower Pace, p. 18.
6. Activities 7 and 9, *Grammar and Vocabulary Workbook,* pp. 5–6
7. Activity 29, p. 18.
8. Have students work in pairs to do Activity 9, *Practice and Activity Book,* p. 7.
9. Presentation: **Comment dit-on… ?,** p. 18
10. Read and discuss **Note Culturelle** and Culture Notes, p. 18.
11. Play the audio recording for Activity 30, p. 19 and check for comprehension.
12. Have students work in pairs or small groups to do Activity 31, p. 19. See also For Individual Needs: Kinesthetic Learners, p. 19.
13. Activity 32, p. 19
    Activity 12, *Practice and Activity Book,* p. 8

Additional Practice Options for Deuxième étape

- *Grammar and Vocabulary Workbook,* pp. 6–8
- *Practice and Activity Book,* pp. 7–10
- Communicative Activities 1-2A and 1-2B, *Activities for Communication,* pp. 3–4
- Situations 1-2 and 1-3: Interview and Role-play, *Activities for Communication,* pp. 89–90
- Realia 1-2, *Activities for Communication,* pp. 52–53
- Additional Listening Activities 1-4, 1-5, and 1-6, *Listening Activities,* pp. 8–9 (Audio CD 1)
- *Interactive CD-ROM Program* (Disc 1)
- *Teaching Transparency 1-2, Teaching Transparencies*
- Additional Grammar Practice, *Pupil's Edition,* Activity 6, p. R54

Close

Close, p. 19

Assess

Quiz 1-2A, Quiz 1-2B, *Testing Program,* pp. 5–8, and/or Performance Assessment, *Annotated Teacher's Edition,* p. 19

STANDARDS FOR FOREIGN LANGUAGE LEARNING

Deuxième étape *Pupil's Edition:* (1.1; 1.2; 1.3; 2.2; 3.1; 3.2; 4.2; 5.2) *Annotated Teacher's Edition:* (1.1; 1.2; 1.3; 2.1; 2.2)

France, les régions

Ending the Chapter (pp. 20–27)

Activities in the shaded boxes enhance the basic lesson and are ideal for **block scheduling**.

Lesson Plans

Lisons!

Objectives
Students will learn to identify the point of view of the narrator.

Prereading
- Motivating Activity, p. 20
- Read and discuss **De bon conseils**, p. 20.
- Activities A and B, p. 20. See the related Teaching Suggestions, p. 20.

Reading
- Activities C–I, pp. 20–21. See Teaching Suggestion, p. 20, and Slower Pace G, p. 21.
- Have students work in pairs to do Activities J–M, pp. 21–22.

Postreading
- Activities N–Q, p. 22. See Literature Link and Thinking Critically, p. 22.
- For Individual Needs: Challenge/Tactile Learners, p. 22

Ecrivons!

Objectives
Students will learn to write for a specific purpose.

- Motivating Activity, p. 23
- Read and discuss **De bons conseils**, p. 23.
- Activity A (**Prewriting**), Activity B (**Writing**), and Activity C (**Postwriting**), p. 23.

Mise en pratique

Objectives
Students will review and integrate all four skills and cultural information in preparation for the Chapter Test.

- Activities 1 and 2, p. 24. See For Individual Needs: Slower Pace, p. 24.
- Read the letter and menus on page 24 aloud, and then have students do Activity 3.
- Play the audio recording for Activity 5, p. 25 and check for comprehension.
- Activity 4, p. 25. See the related Teaching Suggestion, p. 25.
- Have students do **Que sais-je?**, p. 26, individually or with a partner.

Assessment
- Chapter Test, *Testing Program*, pp. 9–14
- *Test Generator*, Chapter 1
- Performance: **Jeu de rôle**, *Pupil's Edition*, p. 25
- Project: **Les régions de la France**, *Annotated Teacher's Edition*, p. 3I
- For alternative assessment options, see the *Alternative Assessment Guide*, pp. 16 and 30.

STANDARDS FOR FOREIGN LANGUAGE LEARNING

Lisons! *Pupil's Edition:* (1.2; 3.1) *Annotated Teacher's Edition:* (1.2; 1.3; 3.1; 4.2)
Ecrivons! *Pupil's Edition:* (1.2; 1.3; 5.1; 5.2) *Annotated Teacher's Edition:* (1.3)
Mise en pratique *Pupil's Edition:* (1.1; 1.2; 1.3; 3.1; 3.2; 4.2; 5.1; 5.2) *Annotated Teacher's Edition:* (1.1; 1.2; 1.3; 2.2; 3.1)

CHAPITRE 2

Belgique, nous violà!

Beginning the Chapter (pp. 28–32)

Activities in the shaded boxes enhance the basic lesson and are ideal for **block scheduling**.

Lesson Plans

Chapter Opener

- Motivating Activity, p. 28
- Teaching Suggestions and Thinking Critically: Comparing and Contrasting, p. 28
- Photo Flash!, pp. 28–29
- Culture Note, Focusing on Outcomes, and Building on Previous Skills, p. 29

Mise en train

Objectives
Students will listen to Hervé and Stéphane, who are on their way to the comic book museum in Brussels.

- Motivating Activity, p. 30
- Presentation: **En route pour Bruxelles,** p. 30 (Audio CD 2). See the related Teaching Suggestion, Culture Notes, and Language Notes, p. 31.
- Math Link, p. 31
- Activities 2 and 3, p. 32. See For Individual Needs: Auditory Learners, p. 32.
- Have students rephrase the sentences in Activity 2 in the **passé composé.**
- Activities 4 and 5, p. 32. See the corresponding Teaching Suggestion and For Individual Needs: Slower Pace, p. 32.
- Have students work in pairs to do Activity 6, p. 32. See the related Teaching Suggestion, p. 32.
- Activity 1, *Practice and Activity Book,* p. 13
- At this time, you may wish to show *Camille et compagnie, Deuxième Épisode : Allez, en route!* (Videocassette 1) as an alternative or in addition to the **Mise en train,** or you may choose to show the video episode at the end of the chapter to review new material.
- Teaching Suggestions and Activities, *Video Guide,* pp. 10 and 12

Resources
For correlated print and audio-visual materials, see *Annotated Teacher's Edition,* pp. 27A–27B.

CHAPITRE 2

STANDARDS FOR FOREIGN LANGUAGE LEARNING
Chapter Opener *Pupil's Edition:* (1.2) *Annotated Teacher's Edition:* (1.2; 1.3; 2.2; 4.2; 5.2)
Mise en train *Pupil's Edition:* (1.2; 1.3) *Annotated Teacher's Edition:* (1.1; 1.2; 1.3; 3.2)

Belgique, nous violà!

Première étape (pp. 33–37)

Activities in the shaded boxes enhance the basic lesson and are ideal for **block scheduling**.

Lesson Plans

Objectives

Students will learn to ask for and give directions, express impatience, and reassure someone.

Motivate

Jump Start! or Motivate, p. 33

Teach

1. Presentation: **Comment dit-on… ?**, p. 33
2. Play the audio recording for Activity 7, p. 33 (Audio CD 2) and check for comprehension.
3. TPR, p. 34
4. Have students work in pairs to do Activities 8 and 9, p. 34.
5. Presentation: **Vocabulaire**, p. 35
6. Play the audio recording for Activity 11, p. 35 (Audio CD 2) and check for comprehension.
7. Activities 2 and 3, *Grammar and Vocabulary Workbook*, p. 10
8. Activity 12, p. 35
9. Game 1, Chapter 2, *Interactive CD-ROM Program* (Disc 1)
10. Presentation: **Grammaire**, p. 35. See Language Notes, p. 35.
11. Activities 13 and 14, p. 36
12. Have students do Activity 15, p. 36, in writing.
13. Presentation: **Comment dit-on… ?**, p. 36
14. Play the audio recording for Activity 16, p. 36 and check for comprehension. See For Individual Needs: Challenge, p. 36.
15. Presentation: **Grammaire** and Activities 17 and 18, p. 37
16. Activities 6 and 7, *Grammar and Vocabulary Workbook*, p. 12

    Game: **Jacques a dit**, p. 37

Additional Practice Options for Première étape

- *Grammar and Vocabulary Workbook*, pp. 9–12
- *Practice and Activity Book*, pp. 14–17
- Communicative Activities 2-1A and 2-1B, *Activities for Communication*, pp. 5–6
- Situation 2-1: Interview and Role-play, *Activities for Communication*, pp. 91–92
- Realia 2-1, *Activities for Communication*, pp. 54, 56
- Additional Listening Activities 2-1, 2-2 and 2-3, *Listening Activities*, pp. 15–16 (Audio CD 2)
- *Interactive CD-ROM Program* (Disc 1)
- *Teaching Transparency 2-1, Teaching Transparencies*
- Additional Grammar Practice, *Pupil's Edition*, Activities 1–4, pp. R55–R56
- **Vidéoclips 1, 2, and 3**, *Video Program* (Videocassette 1). For suggestions and activities, see *Video Guide*, pp. 11 and 14.

Close

Game: Sentence Scrambler, p. 27J

Assess

Quiz 2-1A, Quiz 2-1B, *Testing Program*, pp. 23–26, and/or Performance Assessment, *Annotated Teacher's Edition*, p. 37

STANDARDS FOR FOREIGN LANGUAGE LEARNING

Première étape *Pupil's Edition:* (1.1; 1.2; 1.3; 2.1; 3.1; 3.2) *Annotated Teacher's Edition:* (1.1; 1.2; 1.3; 2.1; 2.2; 3.1; 4.2; 4.3)

CHAPITRE

2

Belgique, nous violà!

Remise en train (pp. 38–40)

Activities in the shaded boxes enhance the basic lesson and are ideal for **block scheduling.**

Lesson Plans

Objectives

Students will listen as Stéphane and Hervé tour the comic book museum in Brussels.

- Motivating Activity, p. 38
- Presentation: **Au centre de la BD,** p. 38 (Audio CD 2)
- Thinking Critically: Drawing Inferences and Teacher Note, p. 39
- Activities 19–22, pp. 38–39
- Have students work in pairs to do Activity 23, p. 39.
- Activities 10 and 11, *Practice and Activity Book,* p. 18
- As an alternative or in addition to the **Remise en train,** you may wish to show *Camille et compagnie, Deuxième Épisode : Allez, en route!* on Videocassette 1 again. For suggestions and activities, see the *Video Guide,* pp. 10 and 12.
- Have students do Activity 24, p. 39 in pairs.
- Pre-viewing suggestions for **Panorama Culturel,** *Video Guide,* p. 10
- Do Presentation: **Panorama Culturel,** p. 40, using *Video Program* (Videocassette 1).
- Post-viewing suggestions for **Panorama Culturel,** *Video Guide,* p. 11
- Culture Notes and Language Notes, p. 40
- Post-viewing Activity 5, *Video Guide,* p. 13
- Read and discuss the questions in **Qu'en penses-tu?,** p. 40.
- Activity 21, *Practice and Activity Book,* p. 24
- **Vidéoclip 4,** *Video Program* (Videocassette 1)
- Viewing Activity 7 and Post-viewing Activity 8, *Video Guide,* p. 14

STANDARDS FOR FOREIGN LANGUAGE LEARNING

Remise en train *Pupil's Edition:* (1.2; 1.3) *Annotated Teacher's Edition:* (1.2; 1.3; 2.2; 3.1; 4.1)

CHAPITRE 2

CHAPITRE 2

Belgique, nous violà!

Deuxième étape (pp. 41–45)

Activities in the shaded boxes enhance the basic lesson and are ideal for **block scheduling.**

Lesson Plans

Objectives
Students will learn to express enthusiasm and boredom and ask and tell where things are.

Motivate
Jump Start! and/or Motivate, p. 41

Teach
1. Presentation: **Comment dit-on… ?**, p. 41. See the related Language Notes, p. 41.
2. Presentation: **Vocabulaire**, p. 41. Read and discuss **A la française**, p. 41.
3. Play the audio recording for Activity 25, p. 41 and check for comprehension.
4. Activity 26, p. 41
5. Activity 12, *Practice and Activity Book,* p. 19
6. Presentation: **Grammaire**, p. 42
7. Activities 12 and 13, *Grammar and Vocabulary Workbook,* pp. 15–16
8. Activity 27, p. 42. See For Individual Needs: Auditory Learners, p. 42.
9. Presentation: **Comment dit-on… ?**, p. 43. See the related Teaching Suggestion and TPR, p. 43.
10. Play the audio recording for Activity 28, p. 43 and check for comprehension.
11. Activity 29, p. 43
12. Have students work in pairs to do Activity 30, p. 45. See the related Teaching Suggestions, p. 45.
13. Motivating Activity and Presentation: **Rencontre Culturelle**, p. 44. See Geography Links and History Link, p. 44.
14. Review **Tu te rappelles?**, and then have students do Activity 31, p. 45. See Additional Practice, p. 45.
15. Have students work in pairs to do Activity 32, p. 45. See the related Teaching Suggestion, p. 45.

Additional Practice Options for Deuxième étape
- *Grammar and Vocabulary Workbook,* pp. 13–17
- *Practice and Activity Book,* pp. 19–22
- Communicative Activities 2-2A and 2-2B, *Activities for Communication,* pp. 7–8
- Situations 2-2 and 2-3: Interview and Role-play, *Activities for Communication,* pp. 91–92
- Realia 2-2, *Activities for Communication,* pp. 55–56
- Additional Listening Activities 2-4, 2-5, and 2-6, *Listening Activities,* pp. 16–17 (Audio CD 2)
- *Interactive CD-ROM Program* (Disc 1)
- *Teaching Transparency 2-2, Teaching Transparencies*
- Additional Grammar Practice, *Pupil's Edition,* Activities 5–9, pp. R56–R57

Close
Close, p. 45

Assess
Quiz 2-2A, Quiz 2-2B, *Testing Program,* pp. 27–30, and/or Performance Assessment, *Annotated Teacher's Edition,* p. 45

STANDARDS FOR FOREIGN LANGUAGE LEARNING
Deuxième étape   *Pupil's Edition:* (1.1; 1.2; 1.3; 2.2; 3.2) *Annotated Teacher's Edition:* (1.1; 1.2; 1.3; 3.1; 4.1; 5.2)

Allez, viens! Level 3

Belgique, nous violà!

Ending the Chapter (pp. 46–53)

Activities in the shaded boxes enhance the basic lesson and are ideal for **block scheduling.**

Lesson Plans

Lisons!

Objectives

Students will learn to preview a reading selection.

Prereading
- Do Motivating Activity, p. 46. Read and discuss **De bon conseils,** p. 46.
- Activities A and B, p. 46. See the related Teaching Suggestions, p. 46.

Reading
- Activities C–G, p. 47. See For Individual Needs: Challenge and Building on Previous Skills, p. 47.
- Activities H–K, p. 48. See For Individual Needs: Visual Learners, Language-to-Language, and the related Teaching Suggestions, p. 48.

Postreading
- Activity L, p. 48. See Group Work, p. 48.
- For additional reading practice, see *Practice and Activity Book,* p. 23.

Ecrivons!

Objectives

Students will learn to identify their audience.

- Prewriting: Motivating Activity, p. 49
- Read and discuss **De bons conseils,** p. 49. See Reading/Writing Link, p. 49.
- Activity A (**Prewriting**), Activity B (**Writing**), and Activity C (**Postwriting**), p. 49. See suggestions to accompany these activities on page 49.
- Compile the comics in a class comic book or in an Internet home page.

Mise en pratique

Objectives

Students will review and integrate all four skills and cultural information in preparation for the Chapter Test.

- Activities 1 and 2, p. 50. See For Individual Needs: Auditory Learners, p. 50.
- Play the audio recording for Activity 3, p. 50 and check for comprehension.
- Activities 4–6, p. 51. See Teaching Suggestion 4 and Language Note, p. 51.
- Have students do **Que sais-je?,** p. 52, individually or with a partner.

Assessment
- Chapter Test, *Testing Program,* pp. 31–36
- *Test Generator,* Chapter 2
- Project: **Le code de la route,** *Annotated Teacher's Edition,* p. 27I
- For alternative assessment options, see the *Alternative Assessment Guide,* pp. 17 and 31.

STANDARDS FOR FOREIGN LANGUAGE LEARNING

Lisons! *Pupil's Edition:* (1.2; 3.1) *Annotated Teacher's Edition:* (1.1; 1.2; 3.2; 4.1)
Ecrivons! *Pupil's Edition:* (1.2; 1.3; 3.2; 5.2) *Annotated Teacher's Edition:* (1.3; 4.1)
Mise en pratique *Pupil's Edition:* (1.1; 1.2; 1.3; 2.2; 3.1) *Annotated Teacher's Edition:* (1.1; 1.2; 1.3; 3.1)

Teacher's Name _____ Class _____ Date _____

Soyons responsables!

Beginning the Chapter (pp. 54–58)

Activities in the shaded boxes enhance the basic lesson and are ideal for **block scheduling.**

Lesson Plans

Chapter Opener

- Motivating Activity and Teaching Suggestions, p. 54
- Photo Flash!, pp. 54–55
- Focusing on Outcomes, p. 55

Mise en train

Objectives

Students will listen as several teenagers ask their parents for permission to do various things.

- Motivating Activity, p. 56
- Presentation: **Je peux sortir?**, p. 57 (Audio CD 3). See the related Language Note, Teacher Notes, and Teaching Suggestion, p. 57.
- Have students work in groups to discuss the questions in Thinking Critically: Analyzing, p. 57.
- Read and discuss **Note Culturelle,** p. 58.
- Activities 1 and 2, p. 58. See For Individual Needs: Kinesthetic Learners, p. 58.
- Play the audio recording for Activity 3, p. 58 and check for comprehension. See For Individual Needs: Challenge 3, p. 58.
- Have students work in pairs to do Activities 4 and 5, p. 58.
- For Individual Needs: Challenge 4, p. 58
- Review the vocabulary for household chores (Level 1, Chapter 7) and the functional expressions to ask for, give, and refuse permission and make excuses (Level 1, Chapters 4 and 5; Level 2, Chapters 5 and 10). Then have students use that material to create a conversation between a parent and a child, based on the models in the **Mise en train.**
- Activity 1, *Practice and Activity Book,* p. 25
- At this time, you may wish to show *Camille et compagnie, Troisième Épisode : Max et l'écologie font bon ménage* (Videocassette 1) as an alternative or in addition to the **Mise en train,** or you may choose to show the video episode at the end of the chapter to review new material.
- For teaching suggestions and activities, see *Video Guide,* pp. 16 and 18.

Resources

For correlated print and audio-visual materials, see *Annotated Teacher's Edition,* pp. 53A–53B.

STANDARDS FOR FOREIGN LANGUAGE LEARNING

Chapter Opener   *Pupil's Edition:* (1.2) *Annotated Teacher's Edition:* (1.3; 2.1; 2.2; 4.1; 5.1; 5.2)
Mise en train   *Pupil's Edition:* (1.2; 1.3; 3.1) *Annotated Teacher's Edition:* (1.2; 1.3; 2.2)

Soyons responsables!

Première étape (pp. 59–63)

Activities in the shaded boxes enhance the basic lesson and are ideal for **block scheduling.**

Lesson Plans

Objectives
Students will learn to ask for, grant, and refuse permission and express obligation.

Motivate
Jump Start! and/or Motivate, p. 59

Teach
1. Presentation: **Vocabulaire,** p. 59. See TPR, p. 59.
2. Play the audio recording for Activity 6, p. 59 (Audio CD 3) and check for comprehension.
3. Activities 3 and 4, *Grammar and Vocabulary Workbook,* p. 19
4. Activities 7 and 8, p. 60. See Building on Previous Skills, p. 60.
5. Presentation: **Comment dit-on… ?,** p. 60
6. Play the audio recording for Activity 9, p. 60 and check for comprehension. See Challenge, p. 60.
7. **Tu te rappelles?,** p. 60. See related Teaching Suggestion.
8. Activity 5, *Grammar and Vocabulary Workbook,* p. 20
9. Presentation: **Grammaire,** p. 61. See the first Additional Practice and Game, p. 61.
10. Activities 10 and 11, pp. 61–62. See the second Additional Practice, p. 61.
11. Activities 9, 11, and 12, *Grammar and Vocabulary Workbook,* pp. 22 and 24
12. Read and discuss **A la française,** p. 62. Then have students work in pairs to do Activity 12, p. 62. Assign partners one situation and have them write and act out the scene.
    Activity 13, p. 62. See For Individual Needs: Slower Pace, p. 62.
13. Presentation: **Vocabulaire,** p. 62. See the related Language Note, p. 63.
14. Activities 14 and 15, p. 63
15. Have students work in pairs to do Activity 16, p. 63.
    Have students work in pairs to do Activity 17, p. 63.
16. Activity 10, *Practice and Activity Book,* p. 29

Additional Practice Options for Première étape
- *Grammar and Vocabulary Workbook,* pp. 18–26
- *Practice and Activity Book,* pp. 26–29
- Communicative Activities 3-1A and 3-1B, *Activities for Communication,* pp. 9–10
- Situation 3-1: Interview and Role-play, *Activities for Communication,* pp. 93–94
- Realia 3-1, *Activities for Communication,* pp. 57, 59
- Additional Listening Activities 3-1, 3-2 and 3-3, *Listening Activities,* pp. 23–24 (Audio CD 3)
- *Interactive CD-ROM Program* (Disc 1)
- Additional Grammar Practice, *Pupil's Edition,* Activities 1–5, pp. R58–R59
- **Vidéoclips 1, 2, and 3,** *Video Program* (Videocassette 1). See *Video Guide,* pp. 17 and 20 for suggestions and activities.

Close
Close, p. 63

Assess
Quiz 3-1A, Quiz 3-1B, *Testing Program,* pp. 45–48, and/or Performance Assessment, *Annotated Teacher's Edition,* p. 63

STANDARDS FOR FOREIGN LANGUAGE LEARNING
Première étape *Pupil's Edition:* (1.1; 1.2; 1.3; 2.1) *Annotated Teacher's Edition:* (1.1; 1.2; 1.3; 3.1; 5.2)

CHAPITRE 3

Soyons responsables!

Remise en train (pp. 64–66)

Activities in the shaded boxes enhance the basic lesson and are ideal for **block scheduling**.

Lesson Plans

Objectives

Students will listen as Isabelle and Gilles go hiking in a park.

- Motivating Activity, p. 64
- Presentation: **Laissez-les vivre!**, p. 65. For now, present only the brochure about camping equipment and hiking rules.
- Language Note, p. 65
- Teaching Suggestion, p. 65
- Play the audio recording of **Laissez-les vivre!**, p. 64 (Audio CD 3). See the first Teaching Suggestion, p. 65.
- Activity 18, p. 64
- Play the audio recording for Activity 19, p. 64 and check for comprehension.
- Activities 20–22, pp. 64–65. See Thinking Critically: Comparing and Contrasting/Analyzing, p. 65.
- Have students work in pairs to do Activity 23, p. 65.
- Activities 11 and 12, *Practice and Activity Book,* p. 30
- Read and discuss **Note Culturelle,** p. 65. See Culture Note and Community Link, p. 65.
- As an alternative or in addition to the **Remise en train,** you may wish to show *Camille et compagnie, Troisième Épisode : Max et l'écologie font bon ménage* on Videocassette 1 again. For suggestions and activities, see the *Video Guide,* pp. 16 and 18.
- Motivating Activity, p. 66
- Presentation: **Rencontre Culturelle,** p. 66
- Language-to-Language, p. 66.
- Read and discuss the questions in **Qu'en penses-tu?,** p. 66.
- Have students read **Savais-tu que... ?,** p. 66.
- History Link and Culture Note, p. 66
- Have students try to find more information about and possibly examples of **romansch.**
- Have students working in small groups discuss stereotypes they might have heard about Switzerland or the Swiss people. Based on information in this chapter, or other information they can acquire, have them figure out possible reasons for the stereotypes.

STANDARDS FOR FOREIGN LANGUAGE LEARNING

Remise en train   *Pupil's Edition:* (1.2; 1.3; 2.2; 3.1; 3.2; 4.2; 5.2)   *Annotated Teacher's Edition:* (1.2; 1.3; 2.2; 3.1; 3.2; 5.2)

CHAPITRE 3

Soyons responsables!

Deuxième étape (pp. 67–71)

Activities in the shaded boxes enhance the basic lesson and are ideal for **block scheduling.**

Lesson Plans

Objectives
Students will learn expressions for forbidding, reproaching, justifying their actions, and rejecting others' excuses.

Motivate
Jump Start! and/or Motivate, p. 67

Teach
1. Presentation: **Comment dit-on… ?,** p. 67
2. Read and discuss **Note de Grammaire,** p. 67.
3. Activity 24, p. 67. See For Individual Needs: Challenge, p. 67.
4. Play the audio recording for Activity 25, p. 67 and check for comprehension.
   Have students do Activity 26, p. 67, in writing.
5. Presentation: **Vocabulaire,** p. 69
6. Play the audio recording for Activity 27, p. 69 and check for comprehension.
7. Activity 28, p. 69
8. Activity 19, *Grammar and Vocabulary Workbook,* p. 27
9. Additional Practice, p. 69
10. Presentation: **Comment dit-on… ?,** p. 70
11. Play the audio recording for Activity 29, p. 70 and check for comprehension.
12. Activity 30, p. 70
13. Have pairs of students do Activities 31 and 32, pp. 70–71. See the related Teaching Suggestion, p. 70.
    Activities 33 and 34, p. 71
14. *Teaching Transparency 3-2.* See the accompanying Teaching Suggestions.
15. Motivating Activity, p. 68
16. Do Presentation: **Panorama Culturel,** p. 68, using the *Video Program* (Videocassette 1).
    Suggestions and activities for **Panorama Culturel,** *Video Guide,* pp. 17 and 19

Additional Practice Options for Deuxième étape
- *Grammar and Vocabulary Workbook,* pp. 27–28
- *Practice and Activity Book,* pp. 31–34, 36
- Communicative Activities 3-2A and 3-2B, *Activities for Communication,* pp. 11–12
- Situations 3-2 and 3-3: Interview and Role-play, *Activities for Communication,* pp. 93–94
- Realia 3-2, *Activities for Communication,* pp. 58–59
- Additional Listening Activities 3-4, 3-5, and 3-6, *Listening Activities,* pp. 24–25 (Audio CD 3)
- *Interactive CD-ROM Program* (Disc 1)
- Additional Grammar Practice, *Pupil's Edition,* Activities 6–7, pp. R59–R60

Close
Close, p. 71

Assess
Quiz 3-2A, Quiz 3-2B, *Testing Program,* pp. 49–52, and/or Performance Assessment, *Annotated Teacher's Edition,* p. 71

STANDARDS FOR FOREIGN LANGUAGE LEARNING
Deuxième étape   *Pupil's Edition:* (1.1; 1.2; 1.3; 2.2; 3.1; 3.2; 4.2; 5.1; 5.2) *Annotated Teacher's Edition:* (1.1; 1.2; 1.3; 3.1; 3.2; 5.1)

CHAPITRE 3

CHAPITRE 3

Soyons responsables!

Ending the Chapter (pp. 72–79)

Activities in the shaded boxes enhance the basic lesson and are ideal for **block scheduling**.

Lesson Plans

Lisons!

Objectives
Students will learn how to derive meaning from context.

Prereading
- Motivating Activity, p. 72
- Read and discuss **De bon conseils,** p. 72.
- Activities A and B, p. 72. See the related Teaching Suggestion, p. 72.

Reading
- Have students read **Albert Nez en l'air** and do Activities C–K, pp. 72–73. See the related Teaching Suggestion, p. 73.
- Have students read **Julie Boum** and do Activities L–P, p. 74. See For Individual Needs: Slower Pace, p. 74.

Postreading
- Activity Q, p. 74. See Reading/Writing Link, p. 74.
- For additional reading practice, see *Practice and Activity Book,* Activity 21, p. 35.

Ecrivons!

Objectives
Students will learn to make an outline before they write.

- Motivating Activity, p. 75. Read and discuss **De bons conseils,** p. 75.
- Activity A **(Prewriting)**, Activity B **(Writing)**, and Activity C **(Postwriting)**, p. 75. See the suggestions to accompany these activities on page 75.

Mise en pratique

Objectives
Students will review and integrate all four skills and cultural information in preparation for the Chapter Test.

- Play the audio recording for Activity 1, p. 76 and check for comprehension.
- Activities 2 and 3, pp. 76–77. See Language Note, p. 76, and Thinking Critically: Analyzing, p. 77.
- Activity 4, p. 77. See the related Teaching Suggestion, p. 77.
- Have students work in pairs to do Activities 5 and 6, p. 77.
- Have students do **Que sais-je?,** p. 78, individually or with a partner.

Assessment
- Chapter Test, *Testing Program,* pp. 53-58
- *Test Generator,* Chapter 3
- Project: L'environnement, *Annotated Teacher's Edition,* p. 53I
- For alternative assessment options, see the *Alternative Assessment Guide,* pp. 18 and 32.

STANDARDS FOR FOREIGN LANGUAGE LEARNING

Lisons! *Pupil's Edition:* (1.2; 1.3; 3.1; 4.1) *Annotated Teacher's Edition:* (1.2; 1.3; 3.1)
Ecrivons! *Pupil's Edition:* (1.3; 5.2) *Annotated Teacher's Edition:* (1.3)
Mise en pratique *Pupil's Edition:* (1.1; 1.2; 1.3; 2.2; 3.1; 3.2; 5.2) *Annotated Teacher's Edition:* (1.2; 1.3; 3.1)

CHAPITRE **4**

Des goûts et des couleurs

Beginning the Chapter (pp. 80–84)

Activities in the shaded boxes enhance the basic lesson and are ideal for **block scheduling**.

Lesson Plans

CHAPITRE 4

Chapter Opener

- Motivating Activity, p. 80
- Teaching Suggestion and Culture Notes, p. 80
- Photo Flash!, p. 80
- Teaching Suggestions and Focusing on Outcomes, p. 81
- History Link, p. 81

Mise en train

Objectives

Students will listen as two teenagers discuss the fashions in a catalogue that arrived in the mail.

- Motivating Activity, p. 82
- Read and discuss Culture Note, p. 83 and **Note Culturelle**, p. 84.
- Presentation: **Mon look, c'est mon affaire**, p. 83 (Audio CD 4). See the related Language Note, p. 83.
- Building on Previous Skills, p. 83
- Activities 1–3, p. 84. See For Individual Needs: Visual/Kinesthetic Learners, p. 84.
- Have students work in pairs to do Activity 4, p. 84. See the related Teaching Suggestion and Language Note, p. 84.
- Activity 5, p. 84
- Have students do Activity 6, p. 84, in writing.
- Replay the audio recording of **Mon look, c'est mon affaire.** Replay at random various remarks the speakers make. Pause after each remark and ask students to explain the context and the purpose of the remark.
- Activity 1, *Practice and Activity Book*, p. 37
- At this time, you may wish to show *Camille et compagnie, Quatrième Épisode : C'est tout à fait toi!* (Videocassette 2) as an alternative or in addition to the **Mise en train,** or you may choose to show the video episode at the end of the chapter to review new material.
- Teaching Suggestions and Activities, *Video Guide,* pp. 22 and 24

Resources

For correlated print and audio-visual materials, see *Annotated Teacher's Edition,* pp. 79A–79B.

STANDARDS FOR FOREIGN LANGUAGE LEARNING

Chapter Opener   *Pupil's Edition:* (1.2) *Annotated Teacher's Edition:* (1.3; 5.2)
Mise en train   *Pupil's Edition:* (1.2; 3.1; 3.2) *Annotated Teacher's Edition:* (1.3; 2.1; 2.2)

Allez, viens! Level 3

Lesson Planner **17**

CHAPITRE 4

Des goûts et des couleurs

Première étape (pp. 85–90)

Activities in the shaded boxes enhance the basic lesson and are ideal for **block scheduling.**

 Lesson Plans

Objectives
Students will learn to ask for and give opinions, ask which one(s), and point out and identify people and things.

Motivate
Jump Start! and Motivate, p. 85

Teach
1. Review **Si tu as oublié,** p. 85.
2. Presentation: **Vocabulaire,** p. 85
3. Game 1, Chapter 4, *Interactive CD-ROM Program* (Disc 1)
4. Play the audio recording for Activity 7, p. 85 (Audio CD 4) and check for comprehension.
5. Activities 4–6, *Grammar and Vocabulary Workbook,* pp. 30–31
6. Present **Vocabulaire à la carte,** p. 86, and then have students do Activities 8 and 9.
7. Presentation: **Comment dit-on... ?** and Reteaching: Object pronouns, p. 86
8. Play the audio recording for Activity 10, p. 86 and check for comprehension.
9. Have students work in pairs to do Activity 11, p. 87.
10. Presentation: **Vocabulaire,** p. 87. See For Individual Needs: Visual Learners, p. 86.
11. Have students do Activity 12 and, in pairs, Activity 13, p. 87.
12. Activity 14 and Additional Practice, p. 88
    Activity 15, p. 88. See the related Teaching Suggestion, p. 88.
13. Presentation: **Comment dit-on... ?,** p. 88. See the related Teaching Suggestion, p. 88.
14. Play the audio recording for Activity 16, p. 88 and check for comprehension.
15. Presentation: **Grammaire** and Additional Practice, p. 89
16. Play the audio recording for Activity 17, p. 89 and check for comprehension.
17. Activities 16 and 17, *Grammar and Vocabulary Workbook,* p. 37
18. Activities 18 and 20, pp. 89–90. See the related Teaching Suggestions, p. 90.
    Activity 19, p. 90

Additional Practice Options for Première étape
- *Grammar and Vocabulary Workbook,* pp. 29–37
- *Practice and Activity Book,* pp. 38–41
- Communicative Activities 4-1A and 4-1B, *Activities for Communication,* pp. 13–14
- Situations 4-1 and 4-2: Interview and 4-1: Role-play, *Activities for Communication,* pp. 95–96
- Realia 4-1, *Activities for Communication,* pp. 60, 62
- Additional Listening Activities 4-1, 4-2 and 4-3, *Listening Activities,* pp. 31–32 (Audio CD 4)
- *Interactive CD-ROM Program* (Disc 1)
- *Teaching Transparency 4-1, Teaching Transparencies*
- Additional Grammar Practice, *Pupil's Edition,* Activities 1–3, pp. R60–R61

Close
Close, p. 90

Assess
Quiz 4-1A, Quiz 4-1B, *Testing Program,* pp. 67–70, and/or Performance Assessment, *Annotated Teacher's Edition,* p. 90

STANDARDS FOR FOREIGN LANGUAGE LEARNING
Première étape *Pupil's Edition:* (1.1; 1.2; 1.3; 2.1; 2.2; 3.1; 3.2; 4.2; 5.2) *Annotated Teacher's Edition:* (1.1; 1.2; 1.3; 3.1)

CHAPITRE

4

Des goûts et des couleurs

Remise en train (pp. 91–93)

Activities in the shaded boxes enhance the basic lesson and are ideal for **block scheduling**.

Lesson Plans

CHAPITRE 4

Objectives

Students will listen as two teenagers try to decide what to wear to a concert.

- Motivating Activity, p. 92
- Read and discuss **Note Culturelle,** p. 93.
- You might have students discuss styles from American and French fashion magazines.
- Review the vocabulary on page 87, and then have students do Activity 4, *Practice and Activity Book,* p. 38, as a review.
- Presentation: **Chacun son style!,** p. 92 (Audio CD 4). See the related Language Note, p. 93.
- Activities 21–23, p. 92
- For Individual Needs: Challenge, p. 93
- Have students work in pairs to do Activity 24, p. 93.
- Activity 25, p. 93. See Thinking Critically: Comparing and Contrasting, p. 93.
- Activities 9 and 10, *Practice and Activity Book,* pp. 41–42
- As an alternative or in addition to the **Remise en train,** you may wish to show *Camille et compagnie, Quatrième Épisode : C'est tout à fait toi!* on Videocassette 2 again. For suggestions and activities, see the *Video Guide,* pp. 22 and 24.
- Do Presentation: **Panorama Culturel,** p. 91, using *Video Program* (Videocassette 2). See the related Language Note, p. 91.
- Teaching Suggestion, p. 91
- Activities 4 and 5, *Video Guide,* p. 25
- Read and discuss the questions in **Qu'en penses-tu?,** p. 91.
- Go over **Questions,** p. 91.
- Activity 22, *Practice and Activity Book,* p. 48

STANDARDS FOR FOREIGN LANGUAGE LEARNING

Remise en train   *Pupil's Edition:* (1.2) *Annotated Teacher's Edition:* (1.2; 2.1; 4.2)

CHAPITRE 4

Des goûts et des couleurs

Deuxième étape (pp. 94–97)

Activities in the shaded boxes enhance the basic lesson and are ideal for **block scheduling**.

Lesson Plans

Objectives

Students will learn to pay and respond to compliments and reassure someone.

Motivate

Jump Start!, Motivate, and Family Link, p. 94

Teach

1. Presentation: **Vocabulaire,** p. 94
2. Play the audio recording for Activity 26, p. 94 and check for comprehension.
3. Activities 20 and 21, *Grammar and Vocabulary Workbook,* p. 39
4. Have students work in pairs to do Activity 27, p. 94. See For Individual Needs: Slower Pace, p. 94.
5. Presentation: **Grammaire,** p. 95. See the related Language Notes, p. 95.
6. Activity 13, *Practice and Activity Book,* p. 43
7. Activities 28 and 29, p. 95. See Additional Practice, p. 95.
8. Game 5, Chapter 4, *Interactive CD-ROM Program* (Disc 1)

    Present **A la française** and see the related Teaching Suggestion, p. 95.
    Activity 30, p. 96. See Building on Previous Skills, p. 96.

9. Motivating Activity and Presentation: **Comment dit-on... ?,** p. 96
10. Play the audio recording for Activity 31, p. 96 (Audio CD 4) and check for comprehension.
11. Have students write out the answers for Activity 32, p. 97. See For Individual Needs: Visual Learners/Challenge, p. 97.
12. Have students work in pairs to do Activity 33, p. 97.

    Have students work in pairs to do Activity 34, p. 97.
    Game: **Chasse au trésor,** p. 79J

Additional Practice Options for Deuxième étape

- *Grammar and Vocabulary Workbook,* pp. 38, 40
- *Practice and Activity Book,* pp. 43–46
- Communicative Activities 4-2A and 4-2B, *Activities for Communication,* pp. 15–16
- Situations 4-2 and 4-3: Role-play and 4-3: Interview, *Activities for Communication,* pp. 95–96
- Realia 4-2, *Activities for Communication,* pp. 61–62
- Additional Listening Activities 4-4, 4-5, and 4-6, *Listening Activities,* pp. 32–33 (Audio CD 4)
- *Interactive CD-ROM Program* (Disc 1)
- *Teaching Transparency 4-2, Teaching Transparencies*
- Additional Grammar Practice, *Pupil's Edition,* Activities 4–6, p. R62

Close

Close, p. 97

Assess

Quiz 4-2A, Quiz 4-2B, *Testing Program,* pp. 71–74, and/or Performance Assessment, *Annotated Teacher's Edition,* p. 97

STANDARDS FOR FOREIGN LANGUAGE LEARNING

Deuxième étape *Pupil's Edition:* (1.1; 1.2; 1.3; 3.1) *Annotated Teacher's Edition:* (1.1; 1.2; 1.3; 5.1)

Des goûts et des couleurs

Ending the Chapter (pp. 98–105)

Activities in the shaded boxes enhance the basic lesson and
are ideal for **block scheduling.**

Lesson Plans

Lisons!

Objectives

Students will learn how to build on what they know.

Prereading
- Motivating Activity, p. 98
- Career Path, p. 98
- Read and discuss **De bon conseils,** and have students do Activities A–D, p. 98.

Reading
- Activities E–H, p. 99. See Challenge and the related Teaching Suggestions, p. 99.
- Activities I–M, p. 100. See Building on Previous Skills, p. 100.

Postreading
- Activity N, p. 100. See Thinking Critically: Analyzing, p. 100.
- For additional reading practice, see *Practice and Activity Book,* Activity 21, p. 47.

Ecrivons!

Objectives

Students will learn to generate ideas by asking questions.

- See **Prewriting:** Motivating Activity, p. 101.
- Read and discuss **De bons conseils,** p. 101.
- Activity A (**Prewriting**), Activity B (**Writing**), and Activity C (**Postwriting**), p. 101. See the suggestions to accompany these activities on page 101.

Mise en pratique

Objectives

Students will review and integrate all four skills and cultural information in preparation for the Chapter Test.

- Play the audio recording for Activity 1, p. 102 and check for comprehension.
- Have students work in pairs to do Activities 2–5, pp. 102–103. See Teaching Suggestions, p. 102.
- Cooperative Learning, p. 103
- Have students do **Que sais-je?,** p. 104, individually or with a partner.

Assessment
- Chapter Test, *Testing Program,* pp. 75–80
- *Test Generator,* Chapter 4
- Situation Cards, *Activities for Communication,* pp. 95–96
- Project: **Un magazine de mode,** *Annotated Teacher's Edition,* p. 79I
- For alternative assessment options, see the *Alternative Assessment Guide,* pp. 19 and 33.

STANDARDS FOR FOREIGN LANGUAGE LEARNING

Lisons! *Pupil's Edition:* (1.2; 2.1; 2.2; 3.1; 3.2) *Annotated Teacher's Edition:* (1.2; 2.1)
Ecrivons! *Pupil's Edition:* (1.3; 4.2; 5.2) *Annotated Teacher's Edition:* (5.1)
Mise en pratique *Pupil's Edition:* (1.1; 1.2; 1.3; 2.1; 2.2; 3.1; 3.2; 5.2) *Annotated Teacher's Edition:* (1.1; 1.3; 2.2; 3.1)

C'est notre avenir

Beginning the Chapter (pp. 106–115)

Activities in the shaded boxes enhance the basic lesson and are ideal for **block scheduling**.

Lesson Plans

CHAPITRE 5

Location Opener

Objectives

Students will learn about famous people, historical events, and places in francophone Africa.

- Motivating Activity and Background Information, p. 106
- Distribute maps of francophone Africa *(Map Transparency 2)* and lists of French-speaking countries and cities. Have students write the names of the countries and cities on their maps.
- Using the Map, Using the Photo-Essay, and Geography Link, pp. 107–109.
- Viewing suggestions, *Video Guide,* p. 27
- Have students watch **Allez, viens en Afrique francophone!**, *Video Program* (Videocassette 2).
- Viewing and Post-viewing Activities, p. 28

Chapter Opener

- Motivating Activity and Photo Flash!, p. 110
- Focusing on Outcomes, Teaching Suggestions, and Language Note, p. 111
- Group Work, p. 110

Mise en train

Objectives

Students will listen as some Senegalese teenagers tell about their plans for the future.

- Motivating Activity, p. 112
- Read and discuss **Note Culturelle** and Culture Note, p. 114.
- Presentation: **L'avenir, c'est demain**, p. 113 (Audio CD 5)
- Language Note, p. 112
- Activities 1–4, p. 114. See the related game, p. 114.
- Have students work in pairs to do Activity 5, p. 114.
- Teaching Suggestions, p. 114
- Activities 1 and 2, *Practice and Activity Book,* p. 49
- At this time, you may wish to show *Camille et compagnie, Cinquième Épisode : L'avenir est à nous* (Videocassette 2) as an alternative or in addition to the **Mise en train,** or you may choose to show the video episode at the end of the chapter to review new material. See Suggestions and activities, *Video Guide,* pp. 30, 32.
- Motivating Activity, p. 115
- Presentation: **Rencontre Culturelle,** p. 115
- Discuss the questions in **Qu'en penses-tu?,** p. 115.
- Read and discuss **Savais-tu que… ?** and Culture Notes, p. 115.

Resources

For correlated print and audio-visual materials, see *Annotated Teacher's Edition,* pp. 109A–109B.

STANDARDS FOR FOREIGN LANGUAGE LEARNING

Location Opener *Pupil's Edition:* (3.2; 4.3) *Annotated Teacher's Edition:* (2.1; 2.2; 3.2; 4.3)
Chapter Opener *Pupil's Edition:* (1.2) *Annotated Teacher's Edition:* (1.3; 2.2; 3.1; 4.1; 5.1; 5.2)
Mise en train *Pupil's Edition:* (1.2; 1.3; 4.2; 5.2) *Annotated Teacher's Edition:* (1.1; 1.2; 1.3; 2.1; 2.2; 5.1; 5.2)

C'est notre avenir

CHAPITRE 5

Première étape (pp. 116–119)

Activities in the shaded boxes enhance the basic lesson and are ideal for **block scheduling.**

Lesson Plans

Objectives
Students will learn to ask about and express intentions and express conditions and possibilities.

Motivate
Jump Start! and Motivate, p. 116

Teach
1. Presentation: **Vocabulaire,** p. 116. See the related Culture Note, p. 117.
2. Play the audio recording for Activity 6, p. 116 (Audio CD 5) and check for comprehension.
3. Activities 1 and 2, *Grammar and Vocabulary Workbook,* p. 41
4. Present the expressions in **Comment dit-on... ?,** p. 117.
5. Play the audio recording for Activity 7, p. 117 and check for comprehension.
6. Language Note, **Tu te rappelles?,** and Reteaching: The subjunctive, p. 117
7. Activity 8, p. 117
8. Activities 5 and 6, *Grammar and Vocabulary Workbook,* pp. 43–44
9. Presentation: **Grammaire,** p. 118. See the related Language Note, p. 118.
10. Game 2, Chapter 5, *Interactive CD-ROM Program* (Disc 2)
11. Activities 10–12, *Grammar and Vocabulary Workbook,* pp. 46–47
12. Activity 9, p. 118 and related Teaching Suggestion.
13. Activity 10, p. 119.
14. Have students work in pairs or small groups to do Activity 11, p. 119.
    Have students work in pairs to do Activity 13, p. 119. See For Individual Needs: Slower Pace, p. 119.
    Family Link, p. 118
    Have students work in pairs to do Communicative Activities 5-1A and 5-1B, *Activities for Communication,* pp. 17–18.
15. Activity 7, *Practice and Activity Book,* p. 51

Additional Practice Options for Première étape
- *Grammar and Vocabulary Workbook,* pp. 41–48
- *Practice and Activity Book,* pp. 50–53
- Situation 5-1: Interview and Role-play, *Activities for Communication,* pp. 97–98
- Realia 5-1, *Activities for Communication,* pp. 63, 65
- Additional Listening Activities 5-1, 5-2 and 5-3, *Listening Activities,* pp. 35–36 (Audio CD 5)
- *Interactive CD-ROM Program* (Disc 2)
- Teaching Transparency 5-1, *Teaching Transparencies*
- Additional Grammar Practice, *Pupil's Edition,* Activities 1–3, pp. R63–R64

Close
Close, p. 119

Assess
Quiz 5-1A, Quiz 5-1B, *Testing Program,* pp. 89–92, and/or Performance Assessment, *Annotated Teacher's Edition,* p. 119

STANDARDS FOR FOREIGN LANGUAGE LEARNING
Première étape *Pupil's Edition:* (1.1; 1.2; 1.3; 4.2) *Annotated Teacher's Edition:* (1.1; 1.2; 1.3; 2.1; 2.2; 5.1; 5.2)

C'est notre avenir

Remise en train (pp. 120–122)

Activities in the shaded boxes enhance the basic lesson and are ideal for **block scheduling**.

Lesson Plans

Objectives

Students will listen as a Senegalese teenager discusses his plans for the future, first with his parents and then with a friend.

- Motivating Activity, p. 120
- Presentation: **Passe ton bac d'abord!**, p. 121 (Audio CD 5)
- Replay the recording of **Passe ton bac d'abord!** Pause the recording after selected questions or statements and have students identify the communicative function or speaker's purpose.
- Activities 14–16, pp. 120–121.
- You might use Activity 15 for listening comprehension by reading the statements aloud as students listen with their books closed.
- Activity 17, p. 121. See the second Teaching Suggestion, p. 121.
- Read Omar's letter on page 121 aloud. See the first Teaching Suggestion, p. 121.
- Thinking Critically: Synthesizing, p. 121
- Activity 12, *Practice and Activity Book,* p. 54
- As an alternative or in addition to the **Remise en train,** you may wish to show *Camille et compagnie, Cinquième Épisode : L'avenir est à nous* on Videocassette 2 again. For suggestions and activities, see the *Video Guide,* pp. 30 and 32.
- Motivating Activity, p. 122
- Pre-viewing suggestion for **Panorama Culturel,** *Video Guide,* p. 30
- Do Presentation: **Panorama Culturel,** p. 122, using *Video Program* (Videocassette 2).
- Viewing and Post-viewing Activities, *Video Guide,* p. 33
- Read and discuss the questions in **Qu'en penses-tu?,** p. 122.
- Teaching Suggestion, p. 122
- Post-viewing suggestions, *Video Guide,* p. 31
- Activity 23, *Practice and Activity Book,* p. 60

STANDARDS FOR FOREIGN LANGUAGE LEARNING

Remise en train *Pupil's Edition:* (1.1; 1.2; 3.1) *Annotated Teacher's Edition:* (1.2; 1.3; 3.1; 4.1; 5.2)

CHAPITRE 5

C'est notre avenir

CHAPITRE 5

Deuxième étape (pp. 123–127)

Activities in the shaded boxes enhance the basic lesson and are ideal for **block scheduling**.

Lesson Plans

Objectives
Students will learn to ask about future plans, express wishes, express indecision, give advice, request information, and write a formal letter.

Motivate
Jump Start! and Motivate, p. 123

Teach
1. Presentation: **Vocabulaire,** p. 123.
2. Read and discuss **De bons conseils,** p. 123.
3. Play the audio recording for Activity 18, p. 123 and check for comprehension.
4. Game 3, Chapter 5, *Interactive CD-ROM Program* (Disc 2)
5. Activity 19, p. 124
6. Present **Vocabulaire à la carte,** p. 124, and then have students do Activity 20, p. 124. Have students do Activity 21, p. 124, in writing.
7. Presentation: **Comment dit-on... ?,** p. 124. See the related Language Note, p. 124.
8. Play the audio recording for Activity 22, p. 125 and check for comprehension.
9. Have students work in pairs to do Activity 23, p. 125.
10. Presentation: **Grammaire,** p. 125. See the related Language Note, p. 125.
11. Activities 24 and 25, p. 126
12. Game: Verb Toss, p. 125
13. Activities 20 and 21, *Grammar and Vocabulary Workbook,* pp. 52–53
14. Activities 18 and 19, *Practice and Activity Book,* p. 57
15. Motivating Activity and Presentation: **Comment dit-on... ?,** p. 126
16. Present **Note de Grammaire,** p. 127. See Music Link, p. 127.
17. Play the audio recording for Activity 26, p. 126 and check for comprehension.
18. Activities 27 and 28, p. 127

Additional Practice Options for Deuxième étape
- *Grammar and Vocabulary Workbook,* pp. 49–53
- *Practice and Activity Book,* pp. 55–58
- Communicative Activities 5-2A and 5-2B, *Activities for Communication,* pp. 19–20
- Situations 5-2 and 5-3: Interview and Role-play, *Activities for Communication,* pp. 97–98
- Realia 5-2, *Activities for Communication,* pp. 64–65
- Additional Listening Activities 5-4, 5-5, and 5-6, *Listening Activities,* pp. 36–37 (Audio CD 5)
- *Interactive CD-ROM Program* (Disc 2)
- *Teaching Transparency 5-2, Teaching Transparencies*
- Additional Grammar Practice, *Pupil's Edition,* Activities 4–6, pp. R64–R65

Close
Close, p. 127

Assess
Quiz 5-2A, Quiz 5-2B, *Testing Program,* pp. 93–96, and/or Performance Assessment, *Annotated Teacher's Edition,* p. 127

STANDARDS FOR FOREIGN LANGUAGE LEARNING
Deuxième étape *Pupil's Edition:* (1.1; 1.2; 1.3; 3.1; 4.2; 4.3; 5.1; 5.2) *Annotated Teacher's Edition:* (1.1; 1.2; 1.3; 4.1; 5.2)

CHAPITRE 5

C'est notre avenir

Ending the Chapter (pp. 128–135)

Activities in the shaded boxes enhance the basic lesson and are ideal for **block scheduling**.

Lesson Plans

Lisons!

Objectives

Students will learn to recognize the **passé simple** and to use context and familiar root words to deduce the meaning of unfamiliar verb forms they may encounter in a reading selection.

Prereading
- Motivating Activity, p. 128. See also Music Link, p. 128.
- Read and discuss **De bon conseils,** p. 128.
- Activities A and B, p. 128. See Geography Link, p. 130.

Reading
- Activities C–K, pp. 128–130. See Teacher Note, p. 129.
- Group Work and For Individual Needs: Challenge, p. 130

Postreading
- Activities L and M, p. 130
- For additional reading practice, see *Practice and Activity Book,* Activity 22, p. 59.

Ecrivons!

Objectives

Students will learn how to use details and structure in persuasive writing.

- See Prewriting: Motivating Activity, p. 131.
- Read and discuss **De bons conseils,** p. 131.
- Activity A (**Prewriting**), Activity B (**Writing**), and Activity C (**Postwriting**), p. 131. See suggestions to accompany these activities on page 131.

Mise en pratique

Objectives

Students will review and integrate all four skills and cultural information in preparation for the Chapter Test.

- Activities 1–4, pp. 132–133. See Building on Previous Skills, p. 132.
- Teaching Suggestions, pp. 132–133
- Have students do **Que sais-je?**, p. 134, individually or with a partner.

Assessment
- Chapter Test, *Testing Program,* pp. 97–102
- *Test Generator,* Chapter 5
- Performance: **Jeu de rôle,** *Pupil's Edition,* p. 133 or Situation Cards, *Activities for Communication,* pp. 97–98
- Project: Career Day, *Annotated Teacher's Edition,* p. 109I
- For alternative assessment options, see the *Alternative Assessment Guide,* pp. 20 and 34.

STANDARDS FOR FOREIGN LANGUAGE LEARNING

Lisons! *Pupil's Edition:* (1.2; 1.3; 2.1; 3.1; 4.2) *Annotated Teacher's Edition:* (2.1; 2.2; 3.2)
Ecrivons! *Pupil's Edition:* (1.3; 2.1; 5.1; 5.2) *Annotated Teacher's Edition:* (1.3; 5.2)
Mise en pratique *Pupil's Edition:* (1.1; 1.2; 1.3; 2.1; 3.1) *Annotated Teacher's Edition:* (1.1; 1.2; 1.3; 3.1; 5.1)

Allez, viens! Level 3

CHAPITRE 6 — Ma famille, mes copains et moi

Beginning the Chapter (pp. 136–140)

Activities in the shaded boxes enhance the basic lesson and are ideal for **block scheduling**.

Lesson Plans

Chapter Opener

- Motivating Activity, p. 136
- Focusing on Outcomes and Teaching Suggestion, p. 137
- Art Link, p. 137

Mise en train

Objectives

Students will listen as a French teenager, who is on vacation with his family in Morocco, meets a young Moroccan.

- Motivating Activity, p. 138
- Teaching Suggestion, p. 139
- Culture Notes and Photo Flash!, p. 139
- Read and discuss **Note Culturelle,** p. 140. See **Note Culturelle:** Synthesizing, p. 140.
- Presentation: **Naissance d'une amitié,** p. 138 (Audio CD 6)
- Activity 1, p. 140
- Activities 2 and 3 and Additional Practice, p. 140
- To extend Activity 2, have students arrange the sentences in chronological order, and then note quotations from the text that support the statements.
- Have students work in pairs to do Activities 4–6, p. 140. See Thinking Critically: Comparing and Contrasting, p. 140.
- Activity 1, *Practice and Activity Book,* p. 61
- As an additional challenge, have students write what Raphaël might enter in his travel journal at the end of his first day in Morocco.
- At this time, you may wish to show *Camille et compagnie, Sixième Épisode : Une étoile est née* (Videocassette 2) as an alternative or in addition to the **Mise en train,** or you may choose to show the video episode at the end of the chapter to review new material.
- Teaching Suggestions and Activities, *Video Guide,* pp. 36 and 38

Resources

For correlated print and audio-visual materials, see *Annotated Teacher's Edition,* pp. 135A–135B.

STANDARDS FOR FOREIGN LANGUAGE LEARNING

Chapter Opener   *Pupil's Edition:* (1.2) *Annotated Teacher's Edition:* (1.3; 2.1; 2.2; 4.1; 5.2)
Mise en train   *Pupil's Edition:* (1.2; 2.1; 2.2; 4.2) *Annotated Teacher's Edition:* (1.2; 1.3; 2.2; 3.2; 4.2)

CHAPITRE 6

CHAPITRE 6

Ma famille, mes copains et moi

Première étape (pp. 141–145)

Activities in the shaded boxes enhance the basic lesson and are ideal for **block scheduling**.

Lesson Plans

Objectives
Students will learn to make, accept, and refuse suggestions, make arrangements, and make and accept apologies.

Motivate
Jump Start! and Motivate, p. 141

Teach
1. Presentation: **Comment dit-on… ?**, p. 141
2. Play the audio recording for Activity 7, p. 141 (Audio CD 6) and check for comprehension.
3. Activity 8, p. 141 and Activity 9, p. 142
4. Presentation: **Comment dit-on… ?**, p. 142
5. Play the audio recording for Activity 10, p. 142 and check for comprehension.
6. Reteaching: Reflexive verbs, p. 142
7. Presentation: **Grammaire**, p. 142. See Language Note, p. 142 and **A la française**, p. 143.
8. Game 2, Chapter 6, *Interactive CD-ROM Program* (Disc 2)
9. Activity 11, p. 142 and Activity 12, p. 143. See For Individual Needs: Challenge, p. 143.
10. Activities 5 and 7, *Grammar and Vocabulary Workbook*, pp. 56–57
    Communicative Activities 6-1A and 6-1B, *Activities for Communication*, pp. 21–22
11. Have students do Activity 13, p. 143, in writing. See Building on Previous Skills, p. 143.
12. Have students work in pairs to do Activity 14, p. 143.
13. Motivating Activity and Presentation: **Comment dit-on… ?**, p. 144
14. Play the audio recording for Activity 15, p. 144 and check for comprehension.
15. Presentation: **Grammaire**, p. 144
16. Activities 16 and 17, p. 144. Have students do Activity 17 in writing.
17. Pre-viewing Activity 4, *Video Guide*, p. 39
18. Do Presentation: **Panorama Culturel**, p. 145, using *Video Program* (Videocassette 2).
19. Read and discuss the questions in **Qu'en pense-tu?**, p. 145.
    Suggestions and Activities for **Panorama Culturel**, *Video Guide*, pp. 36–37, 39

Additional Practice Options for Première étape
- *Grammar and Vocabulary Workbook*, pp. 54–59
- *Practice and Activity Book*, pp. 62–65, 72
- Situation 6-1: Interview and Role-play, *Activities for Communication*, pp. 99–100
- Realia 6-1, *Activities for Communication*, pp. 66, 68
- Additional Listening Activities 6-1, 6-2 and 6-3, *Listening Activities*, pp. 43–44 (Audio CD 6)
- *Interactive CD-ROM Program* (Disc 2)
- *Teaching Transparency 6-1, Teaching Transparencies*
- Additional Grammar Practice, *Pupil's Edition*, Activities 1–3, pp. R66–R67

Close
Close, p. 144

Assess
Quiz 6-1A, Quiz 6-1B, *Testing Program*, pp. 111–114, and/or Performance Assessment, *Annotated Teacher's Edition*, p. 144

STANDARDS FOR FOREIGN LANGUAGE LEARNING
Première étape　*Pupil's Edition:* (1.1; 1.2; 1.3; 3.1; 4.2; 5.2)　*Annotated Teacher's Edition:* (1.1; 1.2; 1.3; 2.1; 3.1; 5.1)

CHAPITRE 6

Ma famille, mes copains et moi

Remise en train (pp. 146–148)

Activities in the shaded boxes enhance the basic lesson and are ideal for **block scheduling**.

Lesson Plans

Objectives
Students will listen as a Moroccan family welcomes a vacationing French family into their home.

- Motivating Activity, p. 146
- Presentation: **Ahlên, merhabîn,** p. 147 (Audio CD 6). Before playing the recording, have students read the questions in Activity 18, p. 144.
- Culture Note, p. 147, and **Note Culturelle,** p. 150
- Activities 19–22, pp. 146–147
- Have students work in pairs to do Activity 23, p. 147
- You might make a contest out of Activity 22, p. 147. Form two teams. The first team to find and repeat aloud the correct expression wins a point.
- Have students work in small groups to do Activity 23, p. 147. See Thinking Critically: Comparing and Contrasting, p. 147.
- Thinking Critically: Analyzing, p. 147
- Activities 9 and 10, *Practice and Activity Book,* p. 66
- As an alternative or in addition to the **Remise en train,** you may wish to show *Camille et compagnie, Sixième Épisode : Une étoile est née* on Videocassette 2 again. For suggestions and activities, see the *Video Guide,* pp. 36 and 38.
- Motivating Activity, p. 148
- Presentation: **Rencontre Culturelle,** p. 148
- Read and discuss the questions in **Qu'en penses-tu?,** p. 148.
- Go over **Savais-tu que… ?** and Culture Note, p. 148.
- For Individual Needs: Challenge, p. 148
- Some students might be interested in investigating the history of the French Foreign Legion and its role in North Africa.
- Realia 6-1 and 6-2, *Activities for Communication,* pp. 66–68

STANDARDS FOR FOREIGN LANGUAGE LEARNING

Remise en train   *Pupil's Edition:* (1.2; 2.1; 4.2; 4.3)   *Annotated Teacher's Edition:* (1.2; 1.3; 2.1; 2.2; 4.2)

CHAPITRE 6

CHAPITRE 6

Ma famille, mes copains et moi

Deuxième étape (pp. 149–153)

Activities in the shaded boxes enhance the basic lesson and are ideal for **block scheduling**.

Lesson Plans

Objectives
Students will learn to show and respond to hospitality, express and respond to thanks, and quarrel.

Motivate
Jump Start!, p. 149

Teach
1. Do Presentation: **Comment dit-on… ?** and read and discuss Career Path, p. 149.
2. Play the audio recording for Activity 24, p. 149 and check for comprehension. See For Individual Needs: Slower Pace, p. 149.
3. Activities 25–27, p. 150. See Additional Practice, p. 150.
4. Situation 6-3: Interview, *Activities for Communication*, pp. 99–100
5. Presentation: **Vocabulaire**, p. 151. See the related Language Notes, p. 151.
6. Play the audio recording for Activity 28, p. 151 and check for comprehension.
7. Game 5, Chapter 6, *Interactive CD-ROM Program* (Disc 2)
8. Activities 13 and 14, *Grammar and Vocabulary Workbook*, pp. 60–61
9. Activity 29, p. 152
10. Cooperative Learning, p. 152
11. Have students work in small groups to do Activity 30, p. 152.
12. Present the expressions in **Comment dit-on… ?**, p. 153. See Teacher Note and **A la française**, p. 153.
13. Play the audio recording for Activity 32, p. 153 and check for comprehension.
14. Activities 14 and 15, *Practice and Activity Book*, pp. 69–70
15. Have students work in pairs to do Activity 33, p. 153.
16. Have students work in small groups to do Activity 34, p. 153.
    Have students work in small groups to do Activity 35, p. 153.

Additional Practice Options for Deuxième étape
- *Grammar and Vocabulary Workbook*, pp. 60–62
- *Practice and Activity Book*, pp. 67–70
- Communicative Activities 6-2A and 6-2B, *Activities for Communication*, pp. 23–24
- Situations 6-2: Interview and Role-play and 6-3: Role-Play, *Activities for Communication*, pp. 99–100
- Realia 6-2, *Activities for Communication*, pp. 67–68
- Additional Listening Activities 6-4, 6-5, and 6-6, *Listening Activities*, pp. 44–45 (Audio CD 6)
- *Interactive CD-ROM Program* (Disc 12)
- *Teaching Transparency 6-2, Teaching Transparencies*
- Additional Grammar Practice, *Pupil's Edition*, Activities 4–6, pp. R67–R68
- Games: **C'est qui, alors?** and **Le football américain**, p. 135J

Close
Close, p. 153

Assess
Quiz 6-2A, Quiz 6-2B, *Testing Program*, pp. 115–118, and/or Performance Assessment, *Annotated Teacher's Edition*, p. 153

STANDARDS FOR FOREIGN LANGUAGE LEARNING
Deuxième étape *Pupil's Edition:* (1.1; 1.2; 1.3; 2.1; 4.1; 4.2) *Annotated Teacher's Edition:* (1.1; 1.2; 1.3; 2.1; 2.2; 3.1; 4.2; 4.3)

CHAPITRE 6

Ma famille, mes copains et moi

Ending the Chapter (pp. 154–161)

Activities in the shaded boxes enhance the basic lesson and are ideal for **block scheduling**.

Lesson Plans

Lisons!

Objectives

Students will learn how to take cultural context into account.

Prereading
- Motivating Activity, p. 154
- Read and discuss **De bon conseils,** p. 154.
- Activities A and B, p. 154

Reading
- Have students read **Les Trois Femmes du roi**, and then do Activities C–M, pp. 154–156. See Thinking Critically: Analyzing, G, p. 155.
- Have students read **La Petite Maison**, and then do Activity N, p. 156.

Postreading
- Activities O–Q, p. 156
- Thinking Critically: Synthesizing, p. 156
- For additional reading practice, see *Practice and Activity Book,* Activity 18, p. 71.

Ecrivons!

Objectives

Students will learn how to use graphic devices to organize ideas.

- Read and discuss **De bons conseils,** p. 157.
- Activity A **(Prewriting)**, Activity B **(Writing)**, and Activity C **(Postwriting)**, p. 157. See the suggestions to accompany these activities on page 157.

Mise en pratique

Objectives

Students will review and integrate all four skills and cultural information in preparation for the Chapter Test.

- Play the audio recording for Activity 1, p. 158 and check for comprehension.
- For Individual Needs: Challenge, p. 158
- Activities 2–5, p. 159. See the related Teaching Suggestion, p. 159.
- Have students do **Que sais-je?,** p. 160, individually or with a partner.

Assessment
- Chapter Test, *Testing Program,* pp. 119–124
- *Test Generator,* Chapter 6
- **Jeu de rôle,** *Pupil's Edition,* p. 159 or Situation Cards, *Activities for Communication,* pp. 99–100
- Project: **Une publicité pour le Maroc,** *Annotated Teacher's Edition,* p. 135I
- For alternative assessment options, see the *Alternative Assessment Guide,* pp. 21 and 35.

STANDARDS FOR FOREIGN LANGUAGE LEARNING

Lisons! *Pupil's Edition:* (1.2; 2.1; 4.2) *Annotated Teacher's Edition:* (1.3; 2.1; 2.2; 4.2)

Ecrivons! *Pupil's Edition:* (1.3; 5.2) *Annotated Teacher's Edition:* (1.3)

Mise en pratique *Pupil's Edition:* (1.1; 1.2; 1.3; 2.1; 3.1; 4.2) *Annotated Teacher's Edition:* (1.2; 1.3; 2.2; 3.1)

CHAPITRE 6

CHAPITRE 7

Un safari-photo

Beginning the Chapter (pp. 162–167)

Activities in the shaded boxes enhance the basic lesson and are ideal for **block scheduling.**

Lesson Plans

Chapter Opener

- Motivating Activity, p. 162
- Teaching Suggestion, p. 162. Have students work in small groups to brainstorm what they know about Africa, and then share their thoughts with the rest of the class.
- Photo Flash! and Geography Link, p. 162
- Focusing on Outcomes, p. 163
- Teaching Suggestion, Culture Note, and Math Link, p. 163

Mise en train

Objectives

Students will listen as Lucie and her brother Joseph persuade their father to take them on a photo safari in the Central African Republic.

- Motivating Activity, p. 164
- Read and discuss **Note Culturelle,** p. 166.
- Presentation: **Un safari, ça se prépare!,** p. 165 (Audio CD 7).
- Culture Notes, p. 165
- Teaching Suggestion, p. 165
- Activities 1–4, p. 166. See For Individual Needs: Challenge, p. 166.
- Have students work in pairs to do Activities 5 and 6, p. 166. See the related For Individual Needs: Auditory Learners, p. 166.
- Activity 1, *Practice and Activity Book,* p. 73
- At this time, you may wish to show *Camille et compagnie, Septième Épisode : Nos amies les bêtes* (Videocassette 3) as an alternative or in addition to the **Mise en train,** or you may choose to show the video episode at the end of the chapter to review new material.
- Teaching Suggestions and Activities, *Video Guide,* pp. 42 and 44
- Motivating Activity, p. 167
- Read and discuss the questions in **Qu'en penses-tu?,** p. 167.
- Presentation: **Rencontre Culturelle,** p. 167. See the related Teaching Suggestion, p. 167.
- History Link, Language Note, and Culture Notes, p. 167
- Some students might like to read Joseph Conrad's *Heart of Darkness* or Thomas Pakenham's *The Scramble for Africa.* Before you assign these readings, you might wish to preview the books to determine if they are appropriate for your students.

Resources

For correlated print and audio-visual materials, see *Annotated Teacher's Edition,* pp. 161A–161B.

STANDARDS FOR FOREIGN LANGUAGE LEARNING

Chapter Opener   *Pupil's Edition:* (1.2) *Annotated Teacher's Edition:* (1.3; 2.1; 3.2)
Mise en train   *Pupil's Edition:* (1.2; 1.3) *Annotated Teacher's Edition:* (1.2; 2.1; 3.2)

Allez, viens! Level 3

7 Un safari-photo

Première étape (pp. 168–173)

Activities in the shaded boxes enhance the basic lesson and are ideal for **block scheduling.**

Lesson Plans

Objectives
Students will learn to make suppositions, express doubt and certainty, and ask for and give advice.

Motivate
Jump Start! and Motivate, p. 168

Teach
1. Presentation: **Vocabulaire,** p. 168
2. Play the audio recording for Activity 7, p. 168 (Audio CD 7) and check for comprehension.
3. Game 1, Chapter 7, *Interactive CD-ROM Program* (Disc 2)
4. Have students work in pairs to do Activity 8, p. 168, and then read their completed conversations aloud.
5. Activities 2 and 3, *Grammar and Vocabulary Workbook,* pp. 63–64
6. Presentation: **Comment dit-on... ?,** p. 169. See Reteaching: The subjunctive, p. 169.
7. Play the audio recording for Activity 9, p. 169 and check for comprehension.
8. Have students work in pairs to do Activity 10, p. 169.
9. Presentation: **Vocabulaire,** p. 170. See TPR and Additional Practice, p. 170.
10. Play the audio recording for Activity 11, p. 170 and check for comprehension.
11. Activity 12, p. 170
12. Presentation: **Comment dit-on... ?,** p. 171. See the related Teacher Note, p. 171.
13. Play the audio recording for Activity 13, p. 171 and check for comprehension.
    For Individual Needs: Challenge, p. 171
14. Activity 14, p. 171
15. Presentation: **Grammaire** and Activity 15, p. 172
16. Activities 4 and 5, *Practice and Activity Book,* pp. 75–76
17. Have students work in pairs to do Activity 16, p. 172.
18. Motivating Activity and Presentation: **Panorama Culturel,** p. 173, *Video Program* (Videocassette 3)
    Suggestions and Activities for **Panorama Culturel,** *Video Guide,* pp. 42–43, 45

Additional Practice Options for Première étape
- *Grammar and Vocabulary Workbook,* pp. 63–68
- *Practice and Activity Book,* pp. 74–77, 84
- Communicative Activities 7-1A and 7-1B, *Activities for Communication,* pp. 25–26
- Situation 7-1: Interview and Role-play, *Activities for Communication,* pp. 101–102
- Realia 7-1, *Activities for Communication,* pp. 69, 71
- Additional Listening Activities 7-1, 7-2 and 7-3, *Listening Activities,* pp. 55–56 (Audio CD 7)
- *Interactive CD-ROM Program* (Disc 2)
- *Teaching Transparency 7-1, Teaching Transparencies*
- Additional Grammar Practice, *Pupil's Edition,* Activities 1–3, pp. R68–R69

Close
Close, p. 172

Assess
Quiz 7-1A, Quiz 7-1B, *Testing Program,* pp. 147–150, and/or Performance Assessment, *Annotated Teacher's Edition,* p. 172

STANDARDS FOR FOREIGN LANGUAGE LEARNING
Première étape *Pupil's Edition:* (1.1; 1.2; 1.3; 2.1; 3.1; 3.2; 4.2) *Annotated Teacher's Edition:* (1.1; 1.2; 1.3; 2.1; 2.2; 3.1; 3.2)

CHAPITRE 7

Un safari-photo

Remise en train (pp. 174–175)

Activities in the shaded boxes enhance the basic lesson and are ideal for **block scheduling**.

Objectives
Students will listen as the Zokoue family and their guide go on a photo safari in the Central African Republic.

- Motivating Activity, p. 174
- Culture Note, p. 175
- Presentation: **Le safari, c'est l'aventure!**, p. 175 (Audio CD 7)
- Have students describe the attitudes of the family members in this situation and give examples as they did in the **Mise en train** (Teaching Suggestion, p. 165). Have their attitudes changed?
- Replay the audio recording of **Le safari, c'est l'aventure!** Play different speakers' remarks at random. Have students identify the speaker, to whom the speaker is talking, and the context of the remark.
- Activities 17–19, pp. 174–175
- Have students work in pairs to do Activity 20, p. 175.
- Group Work, p. 175
- Once students have found the communicative expressions in Activity 20, have them take turns saying something in French that would normally elicit each expression. Their remarks may reflect situations other than a safari.
- Activity 9, *Practice and Activity Book*, p. 78
- Have students work in small groups to do Activity 21, p. 175. Have groups share their answers with each other.
- As an alternative or in addition to the **Remise en train,** you may wish to show *Camille et compagnie, Septième Épisode : Nos amies les bêtes* on Videocassette 3 again. For suggestions and activities, see the *Video Guide*, pp. 42 and 44.
- If you can procure a copy of **Le Lion,** a novel by Joseph Kessel that is set in Africa among the Masai people of Kenya and Tanzania, you might enjoy reading excerpts of it to your students.

STANDARDS FOR FOREIGN LANGUAGE LEARNING
Remise en train   *Pupil's Edition:* (1.2; 1.3) *Annotated Teacher's Edition:* (1.2; 1.3; 2.2)

CHAPITRE 7

Un safari-photo

Deuxième étape (pp. 176–179)

Activities in the shaded boxes enhance the basic lesson and are ideal for **block scheduling.**

Lesson Plans

Objectives

Students will learn to express astonishment, caution someone, express fear, reassure someone, and express relief.

Motivate

Jump Start! and Motivate, p. 176

Teach

1. Presentation: **Vocabulaire,** p. 176
2. Activity 22, p. 176. See Poetry Link, p. 176.
3. Present **Vocabulaire à la carte,** p. 176 and then have students do Activity 23, p. 177.
4. Have students work in pairs to do Activity 24, p. 177.
5. Presentation: **Comment dit-on… ?,** p. 177
6. Read and discuss **A la française,** p. 177.
7. Play the audio recording for Activity 25, p. 177 and check for comprehension.
8. Have students do Activity 26, p. 177, in writing. See the related Teaching Suggestion, p. 177.
   Review **Si tu as oublié,** p. 177, and then have students do Activity 27 in writing.
9. Presentation: **Comment dit-on… ?,** p. 178
10. Play the audio recording for Activity 28, p. 178 and check for comprehension.
11. Activities 29 and 30, p. 178. See For Individual Needs: Challenge, p. 178.
    Teaching Suggestion for Activity 30, p. 178
12. Presentation: **Grammaire,** p. 179
13. Activity 31, p. 179. See the related Teaching Suggestion, p. 179.
14. Activities 15 and 16, *Grammar and Vocabulary Workbook,* p. 72
15. Game 6, Chapter 7, *Interactive CD-ROM Program* (Disc 2)
    Have students work in groups to do Activity 32, p. 179. You might want to videotape each group's scene or the best scene(s).
16. Situation 7-3: Role-play, *Activities for Communication,* pp. 101–102

Additional Practice Options for Deuxième étape

- *Grammar and Vocabulary Workbook,* pp. 69–72
- *Practice and Activity Book,* pp. 79–82
- Communicative Activities 7-2A and 7-2B, *Activities for Communication,* pp. 27–28
- Situations 7-2, 7-3: Interview and 7-2: Role-play, *Activities for Communication,* pp. 101–102
- Realia 7-2, *Activities for Communication,* pp. 70–71
- Additional Listening Activities 7-4, 7-5, and 7-6, *Listening Activities,* pp. 56–57 (Audio CD 7)
- *Interactive CD-ROM Program* (Disc 2)
- *Teaching Transparency 7-2, Teaching Transparencies*
- Additional Grammar Practice, *Pupil's Edition,* Activities 4–6, p. R70

Close

Close, p. 179

Assess

Quiz 7-2A, Quiz 7-2B, *Testing Program,* pp. 151–154, and/or Performance Assessment, *Annotated Teacher's Edition,* p. 179

STANDARDS FOR FOREIGN LANGUAGE LEARNING

Deuxième étape   *Pupil's Edition:* (1.1; 1.2; 1.3; 3.1; 3.2; 5.2)   *Annotated Teacher's Edition:* (1.2; 1.3; 5.1; 5.2)

7 Un safari-photo

Ending the Chapter (pp. 180–187)

Activities in the shaded boxes enhance the basic lesson and are ideal for **block scheduling.**

Lesson Plans

Lisons!

Objectives
Students will learn to understand linking words.

Prereading
- Motivating Activity, p. 180
- Read and discuss **De bons conseils**, p. 180.

Reading
- Have students read **Le cimetière des éléphants** and do Activities A–J, pp. 180–181.
- Have students read **La tortue et le léopard** and do Activities K–Q, p. 182.

Postreading
- Activity R, p. 182
- Thinking Critically: Comparing and Contrasting, p. 182
- For additional reading practice, see *Practice and Activity Book,* Activity 16, p. 83.

Ecrivons!

Objectives
Students will learn to sequence the events of a story.

- Motivating Activity, p. 183
- Read and discuss **De bons conseils**, p. 183.
- Activity A **(Prewriting)**, Activity B **(Writing)**, and Activity C **(Postwriting)**, p. 183. See the suggestions to accompany these activities on page 183.

Mise en pratique

Objectives
Students will review and integrate all four skills and cultural information in preparation for the Chapter Test.

- Activities 1 and 2, p. 184. See Building on Previous Skills, p. 184.
- Play the audio recording for Activity 3, p. 185 and check for comprehension.
- Activities 4 and 5, p. 185
- Have students do **Que sais-je?,** p. 186, individually or with a partner.

Assessment
- Chapter Test, *Testing Program,* pp. 155–160
- *Test Generator,* Chapter 7
- Situation Cards, *Activities for Communication,* pp. 101–102
- Project: **Mon safari-photo en république centrafricaine,** *Annotated Teacher's Edition,* p. 161I
- For alternative assessment options, see the *Alternative Assessment Guide,* pp. 22 and 36.

STANDARDS FOR FOREIGN LANGUAGE LEARNING

Lisons! *Pupil's Edition:* (1.2; 3.1) *Annotated Teacher's Edition:* (1.1; 1.2; 1.3; 2.2)

Ecrivons! *Pupil's Edition:* (1.3; 3.2; 5.2) *Annotated Teacher's Edition:* (1.3; 5.1)

Mise en pratique *Pupil's Edition:* (1.1; 1.2; 1.3; 2.2; 3.1; 3.2; 5.1; 5.2) *Annotated Teacher's Edition:* (1.1; 1.2; 1.3; 2.1; 2.2; 3.1)

La Tunisie, pays de contrastes

CHAPITRE **8**

Beginning the Chapter (pp. 188–193)

Activities in the shaded boxes enhance the basic lesson and are ideal for **block scheduling.**

Lesson Plans

Chapter Opener

- Motivating Activity, Photo Flash, and Culture Notes, p. 188
- Thinking Critically: Observing and Culture Notes, p. 189
- Teaching Suggestions and Focusing on Outcomes, p. 189

Mise en train

Objectives
Students will listen as Zohra, a Tunisian teenager, reads aloud a letter she has written to her cousin Aïcha.

- Motivating Activity, p. 190
- Read and discuss Language Note, p. 191.
- Presentation: **Bisous de Nefta,** p. 191 (Audio CD 8)
- Ask students to find the answers to these questions as they listen to the recording.
    Why does Zohra write to her cousin?
    Why can't Zohra go to Tunis to visit Aïcha?
    What will the girls do in Nefta?
    What is Zohra's ambition?
    How do her mother's wishes differ from Zohra's?
    Who is Mustafa?
    Why does Zohra envy Aïcha?
- Culture Notes and Thinking Critically: Synthesizing, p. 191
- Activities 1–4, p. 192
- Have students work in small groups to do Activity 5, p. 192. See the related Game, p. 192.
- Have students work in pairs to do Activity 6, p. 192.
- Thinking Critically: Comparing and Contrasting, p. 192
- Activity 1, *Practice and Activity Book,* p. 85
- At this time, you may wish to show ***Camille et compagnie**, Huitième Épisode : La Nouvelle Vie d'Azzedine* (Videocassette 3) as an alternative or in addition to the **Mise en train,** or you may choose to show the video episode at the end of the chapter to review new material.
- Teaching Suggestions and activities, *Video Guide,* pp. 48 and 50
- Motivating Activity, p. 193
- Presentation: **Rencontre Culturelle,** p. 193
- Read and discuss the questions in **Qu'en penses-tu?,** p. 193.
- History Link and Language-to-Language, p. 193
- Present Culture Note, p. 193, and **Note Culturelle,** p. 196.
- Teaching Suggestions, p. 193
- Multicultural Link, p. 193

Resources
For correlated print and audio-visual materials, *see Annotated Teacher's Edition,* pp. 187A–187B.

CHAPITRE 8

STANDARDS FOR FOREIGN LANGUAGE LEARNING
Chapter Opener *Pupil's Edition:* (1.2) *Annotated Teacher's Edition:* (1.2; 1.3; 2.1; 2.2; 4.1; 5.1)
Mise en train *Pupil's Edition:* (1.2; 2.1; 4.3) *Annotated Teacher's Edition:* (2.1; 4.2)

La Tunisie, pays de contrastes

CHAPITRE 8

Première étape (pp. 194–199)

Activities in the shaded boxes enhance the basic lesson and are ideal for **block scheduling.**

Lesson Plans

Objectives
Students will learn to ask someone to convey good wishes, close a letter, express hopes or wishes, and give advice.

Motivate
Jump Start! and Motivate, p. 194

Teach
1. Presentation: **Comment dit-on… ?,** p. 194. See the related Teaching Suggestion, p. 194.
2. Play the audio recording for Activity 7, p. 194 (Audio CD 8) and check for comprehension.
   To extend Activity 7, replay the recording and have students tell what wishes are conveyed and why.
3. Have students work in pairs to do Activities 8–10, p. 194.
4. Presentation: **Vocabulaire,** p. 195
5. Activity 11 and Game, p. 195
6. Play the audio recording for Activity 12, p. 196 and check for comprehension.
7. Activity 13, p. 196. See Literature Link and History Link, p. 196.
8. Presentation: **Comment dit-on… ?,** p. 197
9. Play the audio recording for Activity 14, p. 197 and check for comprehension.
10. Activity 8, *Practice and Activity Book,* p. 88
11. Presentation: **Grammaire,** p. 197 and Activities 15–17, pp. 197–198
    To extend Activity 17, have students reread the letters in Chapter 6, Activity 29, p. 152, and tell what they would do in each case.
12. Game 3, Chapter 8, *Interactive CD-ROM Program* (Disc 2)
13. Activity 19, p. 198
14. Do Motivating Activity and Presentation: **Panorama Culturel,** p. 199, using *Video Program* (Videocassette 3).
    Suggestions and activities for **Panorama Culturel,** *Video Guide,* pp. 48–49, 51

Additional Practice Options for Première étape
- *Grammar and Vocabulary Workbook,* pp. 73–77
- *Practice and Activity Book,* pp. 86–89, 96
- Communicative Activities 8-1A and 8-1B, *Activities for Communication,* pp. 30–31
- Situation 8-1: Interview and Role-play, *Activities for Communication,* pp. 103–104
- Realia 8-1, *Activities for Communication,* pp. 72, 74
- Additional Listening Activities 8-1, 8-2 and 8-3, *Listening Activities,* pp. 63–64 (Audio CD 8)
- *Interactive CD-ROM Program* (Disc 2)
- *Teaching Transparency 8-1, Teaching Transparencies*
- Additional Grammar Practice, *Pupil's Edition,* Activities 1–3, pp. R71–R72

Close
Close, p. 198

Assess
Quiz 8-1A, Quiz 8-1B, *Testing Program,* pp. 169–172, and/or Performance Assessment, *Annotated Teacher's Edition,* p. 198

STANDARDS FOR FOREIGN LANGUAGE LEARNING
Première étape *Pupil's Edition:* (1.1; 1.2; 1.3; 2.1; 2.2; 3.1; 3.2; 4.1; 4.2; 4.3) *Annotated Teacher's Edition:* (1.2; 1.3; 2.2; 3.1; 3.2; 4.3)

La Tunisie, pays de contrastes

CHAPITRE 8

Remise en train (pp. 200–201)

Activities in the shaded boxes enhance the basic lesson and are ideal for **block scheduling**.

Lesson Plans

Objectives
Students will listen as Aïcha reads aloud her reply to her cousin Zohra's letter.

- Have students reread Zohra's letter, **Mise en train,** pp. 190–191.
- Presentation: **Salut de Tunis,** p. 201 (Audio CD 8)
- First, ask students to listen carefully to discover the advantages and the disadvantages of Tunis that Aïcha describes. Then play her letter from the beginning through **... cette animation!** Next, ask students to listen further to identify what Aïcha wants Zohra to do, and what Aïcha will do to help her. Then play the letter from **... cette animation!** through **... Ben, ça, on verra!** Now, tell students to listen to the rest of the letter and be able to describe Aïcha's relationship with Chakib and tell why she cannot visit Zohra.
- Activities 21–23, pp. 200–201
- Have students work in pairs to do Activity 24, p. 201. See For Individual Needs: Challenge, p. 201.
- To extend Activity 24, have students choose a real or imaginary correspondent who lives under different circumstances in a different climate. Then have them rewrite the first page of Aïcha's letter, making all the necessary changes to adapt it to their situation.
- Activities 11 and 12, *Practice and Activity Book,* p. 90
- Type a condensed version of Aïcha's letter with the sentences in scrambled order. Distribute copies and have partners rewrite the letter, putting the sentences in correct sequence.
- As an alternative or in addition to the **Remise en train,** you may wish to show *Camille et compagnie, Huitième Épisode : La Nouvelle Vie d'Azzedine* on Videocassette 3 again. For suggestions and activities, see the *Video Guide,* pp. 48 and 50.
- Have students watch **Vidéoclip 2,** *Video Program* (Videocassette 3).
- Viewing Activity 6, *Video Guide,* p. 52
- Post-viewing suggestion, *Video Guide,* p. 49

CHAPITRE 8

STANDARDS FOR FOREIGN LANGUAGE LEARNING
Remise en train *Pupil's Edition:* (1.2; 1.3; 2.1) *Annotated Teacher's Edition:* (1.2; 1.3; 2.2; 5.2)

CHAPITRE 8

La Tunisie, pays de contrastes

Deuxième étape (pp. 202–205)

Activities in the shaded boxes enhance the basic lesson and are ideal for **block scheduling**.

Lesson Plans

Objectives
Students will learn to complain, express annoyance, and make comparisons.

Motivate
Jump Start! and Motivate, p. 202

Teach
1. Presentation: **Vocabulaire,** p. 202. See Game: **Mots associés,** p. 202.
2. Play the audio recording for Activity 25, p. 202 and check for comprehension.
   To extend Activity 25, have students jot down a word that justifies their answer choice as they listen to the recording.
3. Activity 26, p. 202
4. Activity 13, *Practice and Activity Book,* p. 91
5. Motivating Activity and Presentation: **Comment dit-on... ?,** p. 203
6. Read and discuss **A la française,** p. 203. Then play the audio recording for Activity 28, p. 203.
7. Play the audio recording for Activity 27, p. 203 and check for comprehension.
8. Additional Practice, p. 203
9. Activities 29 and 30, p. 203.
10. Presentation: **Comment dit-on... ?,** p. 204
11. Activity 31, p. 204
12. Presentation: **Grammaire,** p. 204. See Additional Practice, Teaching Suggestion, and Music Link, p. 204.
13. Activities 15 and 16, *Grammar and Vocabulary Workbook,* p. 81
14. Game 6, Chapter 8, *Interactive CD-ROM Program* (Disc 2)
15. Activity 32, p. 205
16. Have students do Activity 34, p. 205, in writing.
    Group Work, p. 205
    Activity 35, p. 205

Additional Practice Options for Deuxième étape
- *Grammar and Vocabulary Workbook,* pp. 78–81
- *Practice and Activity Book,* pp. 91–94
- Communicative Activities 8-2A and 8-2B, *Activities for Communication,* pp. 32–33
- Situations 8-2 and 8-3: Interview and Role-play, *Activities for Communication,* pp. 103–104
- Realia 8-2, *Activities for Communication,* pp. 72–73
- Additional Listening Activities 8-4, 8-5, and 8-6, *Listening Activities,* pp. 64–65 (Audio CD 8)
- *Interactive CD-ROM Program* (Disc 2)
- *Teaching Transparency 8-2, Teaching Transparencies*
- Additional Grammar Practice, *Pupil's Edition,* Activities 4–6, pp. R72–R73

Close
Close, p. 205

Assess
Quiz 8-2A, Quiz 8-2B, *Testing Program,* pp. 173–176, and/or Performance Assessment, *Annotated Teacher's Edition,* p. 205

STANDARDS FOR FOREIGN LANGUAGE LEARNING
Deuxième étape *Pupil's Edition:* (1.1; 1.2; 1.3; 4.1; 5.2) *Annotated Teacher's Edition:* (1.1; 1.2; 1.3; 2.2; 4.3)

Allez, viens! Level 3

La Tunisie, pays de contrastes

Ending the Chapter (pp. 206–213)

Activities in the shaded boxes enhance the basic lesson and are ideal for **block scheduling**.

Lesson Plans

Lisons!

Objectives
Students will learn how to relate parts of a story to the main idea.

Prereading
- Motivating Activity, p. 206
- Read and discuss **De bons conseils,** and then have students do Activity A, p. 206.

Reading
- Have students read **Enfance d'une fille** and do Activities B–K, pp. 206–208.
- Have students read **Les Tunisiennes en marche** and do Activities L and M, p. 208.

Postreading
- Activity N, p. 208. See History Link, p. 208.
- For additional reading practice, see *Practice and Activity Book,* Activity 20, p. 95.

Ecrivons!

Objectives
Students will learn how to brainstorm.

- Motivating Activity, p. 209
- Read and discuss **De bons conseils,** p. 209.
- Activity A (**Prewriting**), Activity B (**Writing**), and Activity C (**Postwriting**), p. 209. See the suggestions to accompany these activities on page 209.

Mise en pratique

Objectives
Students will review and integrate all four skills and cultural information in preparation for the Chapter Test.

- Activity 1, p. 210. See the related Teaching Suggestion, p. 210.
- Activity 2, p. 211
- Play the audio recording for Activity 3, p. 211 and check for comprehension.
- Activities 4–6, p. 211. See the related Teaching Suggestions, p. 211.
- Have students do **Que sais-je?,** p. 212, individually or with a partner.

Assessment
- Chapter Test, *Testing Program,* pp. 177–182
- *Test Generator,* Chapter 8
- Situation Cards, *Activities for Communication,* pp. 103–104
- Project: **Ma ville, hier et aujourd'hui,** *Annotated Teacher's Edition,* p. 187I
- For alternative assessment options, see the *Alternative Assessment Guide,* pp. 23 and 37.

STANDARDS FOR FOREIGN LANGUAGE LEARNING

Lisons! *Pupil's Edition:* (1.2; 2.1; 3.1; 3.2; 4.2; 4.3) *Annotated Teacher's Edition:* (2.1; 4.2)
Ecrivons! *Pupil's Edition:* (1.3) *Annotated Teacher's Edition:* (1.1; 1.3)
Mise en pratique *Pupil's Edition:* (1.1; 1.2; 1.3; 2.1; 2.2; 3.1; 3.2; 5.2) *Annotated Teacher's Edition:* (1.1; 1.3; 2.2)

CHAPITRE

9

C'est l'fun!

Beginning the Chapter (pp. 214–223)

Activities in the shaded boxes enhance the basic lesson and are ideal for **block scheduling.**

Lesson Plans

Location Opener

Objectives

Students will learn about famous people, historical events, and places in French-speaking areas of the Americas.

- Motivating Activity, p. 214 and Terms in the Almanac, p. 215
- Background Information, History Links, and Culture Note, pp. 214–217
- Using the Photo Essay, pp. 216–217
- Play Jeopardy® using the terms in the Location Opener. For example, you might give the answer, "Cajun people enjoy this spicy sausage." The contestant should ask, "What is **boudin créole**?"
- Use *Map Transparency 3* transparency master, and have students label the French-speaking areas of the Western Hemisphere.
- Pre-viewing and Viewing suggestions, *Video Guide*, p. 53
- Have students watch ***Allez, viens en Amérique francophone!***, *Video Program* (Videocassette 3).
- Viewing and Post-viewing Activities, p. 54; Post-viewing suggestions, p. 53, *Video Guide*
- Have students research the history of the French influence in a French-speaking area of the Americas.

Chapter Opener

- Motivating Activity and Teaching Suggestion, p. 218
- Focusing on Outcomes, p. 219 and Photo Flash!, pp. 218–219

Mise en train

Objectives

Students will listen as Danielle and her brother Fabien disagree about what to watch on TV.

- Motivating Activity, p. 220. Read and discuss **Note Culturelle**, p. 222.
- Review telling official time, using the TV schedule at the top of page 220. See Teacher Note, p. 221.
- Presentation: **La télé, ça se partage**, p. 221 (Audio CD 9). See the related Language Note, p. 221.
- Activities 1–5, p. 222
- For Individual Needs: Challenge, p. 221 and Multicultural Link, p. 222
- Activity 1, *Practice and Activity Book*, p. 97
- At this time, you may wish to show *Camille et compagnie*, *Neuvième Episode : Le Rêve de Sophie* (Videocassette 3) as an alternative or in addition to the **Mise en train**, or you may choose to show the video episode at the end of the chapter to review new material.
- Suggestions and activities, *Video Guide*, pp. 56 and 58
- Presentation: **Rencontre Culturelle**, p. 223 and Motivating Activity, p. 223
- Read and discuss **Savais-tu que… ?** and **Qu'en penses-tu?**, p. 223.
- Thinking Critically: Comparing and Contrasting, p. 223

Resources

For correlated print and audio-visual materials, see *Annotated Teacher's Edition*, pp. 217A–217B.

STANDARDS FOR FOREIGN LANGUAGE LEARNING

Location Opener *Pupil's Edition:* (3.2; 4.3) *Annotated Teacher's Edition:* (2.2; 3.2; 4.3)
Chapter Opener *Pupil's Edition:* (1.2) *Annotated Teacher's Edition:* (1.2; 1.3)
Mise en train *Pupil's Edition:* (1.2; 1.3; 2.2; 3.2; 4.3) *Annotated Teacher's Edition:* (1.2; 2.2; 4.2)

CHAPITRE 9

Allez, viens! Level 3

C'est l'fun!

Première étape (pp. 224–228)

Activities in the shaded boxes enhance the basic lesson and are ideal for **block scheduling**.

Lesson Plans

Objectives
Students will learn to agree and disagree, express indifference, and make requests.

Motivate
Jump Start! and Motivate, p. 224

Teach
1. Presentation: **Vocabulaire,** p. 224. See the related Teaching Suggestion, p. 224.
2. Play the audio recording for Activity 6, p. 224 (Audio CD 9) and check for comprehension.
3. Activities 3 and 4, *Grammar and Vocabulary Workbook,* p. 83
4. Game 1, Chapter 9, *Interactive CD-ROM Program* (Disc 3)
5. Have students work in pairs to do Activities 7 and 8, pp. 224–225. See Game: **Vingt questions,** p. 224.
   Have students do Activity 9, p. 225, in writing.
6. Presentation: **Comment dit-on… ?,** p. 225
7. Play the audio recording for Activity 10, p. 225 and check for comprehension.
8. Have students work in pairs to do Activities 11 and 12, p. 225.
   For Individual Needs: Visual/Auditory Learners, p. 225
9. Presentation: **Vocabulaire,** p. 226. See TPR, p. 226.
10. Activity 13, p. 226
11. Present **Grammaire,** p. 226, and **Note de Grammaire,** p. 227.
12. Activities 14 and 15, p. 227
13. Additional Practice/Music Link, p. 227
14. Activity 8, *Practice and Activity Book,* p. 100
15. Presentation: **Comment dit-on… ?,** p. 227
16. Play the audio recording for Activity 16, p. 227 and check for comprehension.
17. Activities 17 and 18, p. 228
    Have students work in pairs to do Activity 19, p. 228. See the related Teaching Suggestions, p. 228.

Additional Practice Options for Première étape
- *Grammar and Vocabulary Workbook,* pp. 82–86
- *Practice and Activity Book,* pp. 98–101
- Communicative Activities 9-1A and 9-1B, *Activities for Communication,* pp. 33–34
- Situation 9-1: Interview and Role-play, *Activities for Communication,* pp. 105–106
- Additional Listening Activities 9-1, 9-2 and 9-3, *Listening Activities,* pp. 71–72 (Audio CD 9)
- *Interactive CD-ROM Program* (Disc 3)
- Teaching Transparency 9-1, Teaching Transparencies
- Additional Grammar Practice, *Pupil's Edition,* Activities 1–3, pp. R73–R74

Close
Close, p. 228

Assess
Quiz 9-1A, Quiz 9-1B, *Testing Program,* pp. 191–194, and/or Performance Assessment, *Annotated Teacher's Edition,* p. 228

STANDARDS FOR FOREIGN LANGUAGE LEARNING
Première étape *Pupil's Edition:* (1.1; 1.2; 1.3; 3.1; 5.2) *Annotated Teacher's Edition:* (1.1; 1.2; 1.3; 2.2; 3.1)

C
H
A
P
I
T
R
E

9

C'est l'fun!

Remise en train (pp. 229–231)

Activities in the shaded boxes enhance the basic lesson and are ideal for **block scheduling.**

Lesson Plans

CHAPITRE 9

Objectives

Students will listen as Dina and her cousin Fabien try to decide on a film to see, with a little help from her friends.

- Motivating Activity, p. 230
- Presentation: **D'accord, pas d'accord,** p. 231 (Audio CD 9)
- Have students copy the following chart before they hear the recording. Give a brief synopsis of the conversation they are about to hear. Tell them to listen carefully for what the friends think about the four films and fill in the chart. They might just jot down (don't worry about spelling!) a key word or two in French (**très bien, nul, drôle, très bien fait, marrant, ennuyeux,** etc.). Tell them to write an X under a person's name if that person offers no opinion.

	Dina	Fabien	Marie	Adrien
L'Union sacrée *Mon Père, ce héros* *Sidekicks* *Le Grand Bleu*				

- Read aloud or replay the recording of the descriptions of the films at random and have students try to guess which film is being described.
- For Individual Needs: Challenge, p. 231. Ask if students have seen any of these films. If so, have them state whether they agree with (**Je suis d'accord avec…**) or disagree with (**Je ne suis pas d'accord avec…**) the young Canadians.
- Activities 20–23, pp. 230–231. See For Individual Needs: Challenge 21, p. 231.
- Have students work in small groups to do Activity 24, p. 231.
- Activity 11, *Practice and Activity Book,* p. 102
- As an alternative or in addition to the **Remise en train,** you may wish to show *Camille et compagnie, Neuvième Épisode : Le Rêve de Sophie* on Videocassette 3 again. For suggestions and activities, see the *Video Guide,* pp. 56 and 58.
- Motivating Activity, p. 229
- Do Presentation: **Panorama Culturel,** p. 229, using *Video Program* (Videocassette 3).
- Suggestions and activities for **Panorama Culturel,** *Video Guide,* pp. 56–57, and 59
- Activities 20 and 21, *Practice and Activity Book,* p. 108

STANDARDS FOR FOREIGN LANGUAGE LEARNING

Remise en train *Pupil's Edition:* (1.2; 2.2; 3.1; 4.2; 4.3) *Annotated Teacher's Edition:* (1.2; 1.3; 2.2; 3.1; 4.2)

C'est l'fun!

CHAPITRE 9

Deuxième étape (pp. 232–235)

Activities in the shaded boxes enhance the basic lesson and are ideal for **block scheduling**.

Lesson Plans

Objectives
Students will learn to ask for and make judgements, ask for and make recommendations, and ask about and summarize a story.

Motivate
Jump Start! and Motivate, p. 232

Teach
1. Presentation: **Vocabulaire,** p. 232. See the related Teaching Suggestions, p. 232.
2. Activities 25 and 26, p. 232
   To extend Activity 26, have students write a similar synopsis describing a film they've seen.
3. Presentation: **Comment dit-on... ?,** p. 233. See the related Teaching Suggestion, p. 233.
4. Play the audio recording for Activity 27, p. 233 and check for comprehension.
5. Have students work in pairs to do Activity 28, p. 233. See For Individual Needs: Challenge, p. 233.
6. Activity 14, *Practice and Activity Book,* p. 104
7. Have students work in small groups to do Activity 29, p. 233.
8. Presentation: **Comment dit-on... ?,** p. 234
9. Read and discuss **A la française,** p. 235.
10. Have students read the true/false statements for Activity 30, p. 234 and then play the audio recording and check for comprehension.
    Additional Practice or Game: **Quel film?,** p. 234
11. Presentation: **Grammaire,** p. 234. Do Activities 31 and 32, p. 235.
12. Activities 12 and 13, *Grammar and Vocabulary Workbook,* p. 88
13. Game 5, Chapter 9, *Interactive CD-ROM Program* (Disc 3)
14. Have students do Activity 33, p. 235, in writing.
15. Have students work in pairs to do Activity 34, p. 235.

Additional Practice Options for Deuxième étape
- *Grammar and Vocabulary Workbook,* pp. 87–88
- *Practice and Activity Book,* pp. 103–106
- Communicative Activities 9-2A and 9-2B, *Activities for Communication,* pp. 35–36
- Situations 9-2 and 9-3: Interview and Role-play, *Activities for Communication,* pp. 105–106
- Realia 9-1 and 9-2, *Activities for Communication,* pp. 75–77
- Additional Listening Activities 9-4, 9-5, and 9-6, *Listening Activities,* pp. 72–73 (Audio CD 9)
- *Interactive CD-ROM Program* (Disc 3)
- *Teaching Transparency 9-2, Teaching Transparencies*
- Additional Grammar Practice, *Pupil's Edition,* Activities 4–6, pp. R74–R75

Close
Close, p. 235

Assess
Quiz 9-2A, Quiz 9-2B, *Testing Program,* pp. 195–198, and/or Performance Assessment, *Annotated Teacher's Edition,* p. 235

CHAPITRE 9

STANDARDS FOR FOREIGN LANGUAGE LEARNING
Deuxième étape *Pupil's Edition:* (1.1; 1.2; 1.3; 3.1; 3.2; 4.1; 4.2; 4.3; 5.2) *Annotated Teacher's Edition:* (1.1; 1.2; 1.3)

CHAPITRE 9

C'est l'fun!

Ending the Chapter (pp. 236–243)

Activities in the shaded boxes enhance the basic lesson and are ideal for **block scheduling**.

Lesson Plans

Lisons!

Objectives
Students will learn how to visualize what they are reading.

Prereading
- Motivating Activity, p. 236
- Read and discuss **De bons conseils**, p. 236.
- Have students read the synopsis on page 236 and do Activity A, p. 236.

Reading
- For Individual Needs: Auditory Learners, p. 237
- Have students read the scene from **Fierro** and do Activities B–M, pp. 236–238.

Postreading
- Activities N and O, p. 238. See the related Teaching Suggestion, p. 238.
- For additional reading practice, see *Practice and Activity Book,* Activity 19, p. 107.

Ecrivons!

Objectives
Students will learn how to maintain consistency in what they write.

- Motivating Activity, p. 239
- Read and discuss **De bons conseils**, p. 239.
- Activity A **(Prewriting)**, Activity B **(Writing)**, and Activity C **(Postwriting)**, p. 239. See suggestions to accompany these activities on page 239.
- Cooperative Learning, p. 239

Mise en pratique

Objectives
Students will review and integrate all four skills and cultural information in preparation for the Chapter Test.

- Play the audio recording for Activity 1, p. 240 and check for comprehension.
- Activities 2–5, pp. 240–241. See the related Teaching Suggestions, pp. 240–241.
- Have students do **Que sais-je?**, p. 242, individually or with a partner.

Assessment
- Chapter Test, *Testing Program*, pp. 199–204
- *Test Generator*, Chapter 9
- Performance: **Jeu de rôle**, *Pupil's Edition*, p. 241 or Situation Cards, *Activities for Communication*, pp. 105–106
- Project: **Une bande-annonce**, *Annotated Teacher's Edition*, p. 217I
- For alternative assessment options, see the *Alternative Assessment Guide*, pp. 24 and 38.

STANDARDS FOR FOREIGN LANGUAGE LEARNING

Lisons!   *Pupil's Edition:* (1.2; 3.1; 3.2; 4.3) *Annotated Teacher's Edition:* (1.2; 1.3)
Ecrivons!   *Pupil's Edition:* (1.1; 5.2) *Annotated Teacher's Edition:* (1.1; 1.3)
Mise en pratique   *Pupil's Edition:* (1.1; 1.2; 1.3; 2.1; 3.1; 3.2; 5.2) *Annotated Teacher's Edition:* (1.1; 1.3; 3.1)

CHAPITRE 9

CHAPITRE 10

Rencontres au soleil

Beginning the Chapter (pp. 244–249)

Activities in the shaded boxes enhance the basic lesson and are ideal for **block scheduling.**

Lesson Plans

Chapter Opener
• Motivating Activity and Teaching Suggestion, p. 244
• Photo Flash! and Marine Biology Link, p. 244
• Read and discuss **Note Culturelle,** p. 248
• Focusing on Outcomes, Building on Previous Skills, and Geography Link, p. 245

Mise en train

Objectives

Students will listen as two Guadeloupean boys, Pascal and Maxime, talk about scuba diving and then meet two tourists from metropolitan France, Brigitte and Angèle.

• Motivating Activity, p. 246
• Presentation: **La plongée, quelle aventure!,** p. 247 (Audio CD 10)
• When students offer possible explanations of the photos as suggested in the Presentation, accept or reject their explanations, using expressions from Level 2, Chapter 9, p. 228: **Tu as peut-être raison; C'est possible; Evidemment; Je ne crois pas; Ce n'est pas possible; A mon avis, tu te trompes.**
• Replay the recording of **La plongée, quelle aventure!** Ask students to listen carefully to discover what happens between Pascal and Angèle, and what role their friends Maxime and Brigitte play in this situation.
• Teaching Suggestions, p. 247
• Activities 1–5, p. 248. For an alternate way to do Activity 5, see For Individual Needs: Auditory Learners, p. 248.
• Have students work in pairs to do Activity 6, p. 248.
• For Activity 6, have students prepare and act out a scene in which one student tries to meet the other. Have the class vote on the most original conversation starter.
• Activity 1, *Practice and Activity Book,* p. 109
• At this time, you may wish to show *Camille et compagnie, Dixième Episode : C'est pas la mer à boire!* (Videocassette 3) as an alternative or in addition to the **Mise en train,** or you may choose to show the video episode at the end of the chapter to review new material.
• Teaching suggestions and activities, *Video Guide,* pp. 62 and 64
• Motivating Activity, p. 249
• Presentation: **Rencontre Culturelle,** p. 249
• Culture Note, p. 249
• Have students read and discuss the questions in **Qu'en penses-tu?,** p. 249.
• You might also show the video for the Location Opener about Martinique in *Allez, viens!* Level 2, *Video Program* (Videocassette 2) or *Videodisc Program* (Videodisc 2, Side A).
• Suggestions and activities, *Video Guide,* Level 2, pp. 21–22 (*Videodisc Guide,* pp. 34–36)

Resources

For correlated print and audio-visual materials, see *Annotated Teacher's Edition,* pp. 243A–243B.

STANDARDS FOR FOREIGN LANGUAGE LEARNING

Chapter Opener   *Pupil's Edition:* (1.2) *Annotated Teacher's Edition:* (1.3; 2.1; 3.2; 5.1)
Mise en train   *Pupil's Edition:* (1.1; 1.2) *Annotated Teacher's Edition:* (1.2; 1.3; 2.1; 3.1)

Rencontres au soleil

Première étape (pp. 250–255)

Activities in the shaded boxes enhance the basic lesson and are ideal for **block scheduling**.

Lesson Plans

Objectives
Students will learn expressions to brag, flatter, and tease.

Motivate
Jump Start! and Motivate, p. 250

Teach
1. Presentation: **Vocabulaire** and Activity 7, p. 250
2. Play the audio recording for Activity 8, p. 250 (Audio CD 10) and check for comprehension.
   > Game: **Pictionnaire**, p. 251
   > Game 1, Chapter 10, *Interactive CD-ROM Program* (Disc 3)
3. Activities 9 and 10, p. 251
4. Building on Previous Skills and Presentation: **Comment dit-on… ?**, p. 251
5. For Individual Needs: Visual/Auditory Learners, p. 251
   > Additional Practice, p. 251. Encourage partners to respond appropriately.
6. Play the audio recording for Activity 11, p. 252 and check for comprehension.
7. Have students do Activity 12, p. 252, in writing.
8. Building on Previous Skills and **Si tu as oublié**, p. 252
9. Presentation: **Grammaire**, p. 252 and Activities 13–16, p. 253
10. Motivating Activity and Presentation: **Comment dit-on… ?**, p. 254
11. Play the audio recording for Activity 17, p. 254 and check for comprehension.
12. Have students work in pairs to do Activities 18 and 19, p. 254. See For Individual Needs, p. 254.
13. Do Motivating Activity and Presentation: **Panorama Culturel**, p. 255, using *Video Program* (Videocassette 3).
    > Suggestions and activities for **Panorama Culturel**, *Video Guide*, pp. 62–63, 65
    > Activities 21 and 22, *Practice and Activity Book*, p. 120

Additional Practice Options for Première étape
- *Grammar and Vocabulary Workbook*, pp. 89–92
- *Practice and Activity Book*, pp. 110–113
- Communicative Activities 10-1A and 10-1B, *Activities for Communication*, pp. 37–38
- Situation 10-1: Interview and Role-play, *Activities for Communication*, pp. 107–108
- Realia 10-1, *Activities for Communication*, pp. 78, 80
- Additional Listening Activities 10-1, 10-2 and 10-3, *Listening Activities*, pp. 79–80 (Audio CD 10)
- *Interactive CD-ROM Program* (Disc 3)
- *Teaching Transparency 10-1, Teaching Transparencies*
- Additional Grammar Practice, *Pupil's Edition*, Activities 1–4, pp. R75–R76

Close
Close, p. 254

Assess
Quiz 10-1A, Quiz 10-1B, *Testing Program*, pp. 213–216, and/or Performance Assessment, *Annotated Teacher's Edition*, p. 254

STANDARDS FOR FOREIGN LANGUAGE LEARNING
Première étape   *Pupil's Edition:* (1.1; 1.2; 1.3; 2.1; 3.1; 4.2; 4.3) *Annotated Teacher's Edition:* (1.1; 1.2; 1.3; 2.1; 3.1; 3.2; 4.2)

Rencontres au soleil

Remise en train (pp. 256–257)

Activities in the shaded boxes enhance the basic lesson and are ideal for **block scheduling**.

Lesson Plans

Objectives
Students will listen as Joëlle relates the latest gossip in a letter to her friend Marie-France.

- Motivating Activity, p. 256
- Presentation: **Des nouvelles de Guadeloupe,** p. 257 (Audio CD 10)
- See For Individual Needs: Visual Learners, p. 257
- Replay the recording of **Des nouvelles de Guadeloupe.** Pause each time Joëlle is about to introduce a new bit of gossip: **J'y suis allée avec Viviane. Je ne t'ai pas dit?; Au fait, tu savais que Prosper s'était cassé la jambe?; Tu connais la dernière? Figure-toi que Julie, la sœur de Raoul, s'est mariée; Ah, et puis, tu sais la meilleure? Tiens-toi bien. Michel a raté son bac; pour ma part, je n'arrête pas.** Have students try to supply the news during the pause.
- You might have students write Marie-France's reply to Joëlle's letter, responding to each bit of gossip and describing her situation and activities in Lyon.
- For an additional challenge, have students assume the role of Marie-France and write a letter to a friend of hers, relating Joëlle's news.
- Read and discuss **Note Culturelle,** p. 257. Have students discuss examples of social behavior that might be considered rude in the United States.
- Activities 20–25, pp. 256–257. See Language Note and Language-to-Language, p. 257.
- Activity 11, *Practice and Activity Book,* p. 114
- As an alternative or in addition to the **Remise en train,** you may wish to show *Camille et compagnie, Dixième Épisode : C'est pas la mer à boire!* on Videocassette 3 again. For suggestions and activities, see the *Video Guide,* pp. 62 and 64.

STANDARDS FOR FOREIGN LANGUAGE LEARNING

Remise en train   *Pupil's Edition:* (1.2; 1.3) *Annotated Teacher's Edition:* (1.3; 5.1)

CHAPITRE 10

10

Rencontres au soleil

Deuxième étape (pp. 258–261)

Activities in the shaded boxes enhance the basic lesson and are ideal for **block scheduling**.

Lesson Plans

Objectives
Students will learn to express disbelief, show interest, and tell a joke.

Motivate
Jump Start! and Motivate, p. 258

Teach
1. Presentation: **Vocabulaire,** p. 258. See the related Teaching Suggestion, p. 258.
2. Play the audio recording for Activity 26, p. 258 and check for comprehension.
3. Activities 8 and 9, *Grammar and Vocabulary Workbook,* p. 93
4. Activity 27, p. 258
5. Presentation: **Comment dit-on... ?,** p. 259
6. Play the audio recording for Activity 28, p. 259 and check for comprehension.
   For additional challenge, replay the recording for Activity 28 and ask students to note the reason for each call.
7. Discuss **A la française,** p. 261. Then review gestures that students have previously learned. Encourage students to use these gestures in Activity 29, p. 259.
8. Presentation: **Grammaire,** p. 259. See the related Additional Practice, p. 259.
9. Game: **Sentence Scrambler,** p. 260
10. Game 5, Chapter 10, *Interactive CD-ROM Program* (Disc 3)
11. Activities 30 and 31, p. 260
12. Have students do Activity 32, p. 260, in writing.
    Have students work in pairs to do Activity 33, p. 260.
13. Presentation: **Comment dit-on... ?,** p. 261
14. Play the audio recording for Activity 34, p. 261 and check for comprehension.
15. Have students work in pairs to do Activities 35 and 36, p. 261.

Additional Practice Options for Deuxième étape
- *Grammar and Vocabulary Workbook,* pp. 93–95
- *Practice and Activity Book,* pp. 115–118
- Communicative Activities 10-2A and 10-2B, *Activities for Communication,* pp. 39–40
- Situations 10-2 and 10-3: Interview and Role-play, *Activities for Communication,* pp. 107–108
- Realia 10-2, *Activities for Communication,* pp. 79–80
- Additional Listening Activities 10-4, 10-5, and 10-6, *Listening Activities,* pp. 80–81 (Audio CD 10)
- *Interactive CD-ROM Program* (Disc 3)
- *Teaching Transparency 10-2, Teaching Transparencies*
- Additional Grammar Practice, *Pupil's Edition,* Activities 5–6, p. R77

Close
Close, p. 261

Assess
Quiz 10-2A, Quiz 10-2B, *Testing Program,* pp. 217–220, and/or Performance Assessment, *Annotated Teacher's Edition,* p. 261

STANDARDS FOR FOREIGN LANGUAGE LEARNING
Deuxième étape   *Pupil's Edition:* (1.1; 1.2; 1.3; 4.1; 5.1; 5.2)   *Annotated Teacher's Edition:* (1.1; 1.2; 1.3)

Rencontres au soleil

Ending the Chapter (pp. 262–269)

Activities in the shaded boxes enhance the basic lesson and are ideal for **block scheduling**.

Lesson Plans

Lisons!

Objectives
Students will learn to understand literary devices.

Prereading
- Motivating Activity, p. 262
- Read and discuss **De bons conseils**, p. 262.
- Language Arts Link, p. 262
- Activities A–C, p. 262. See the related Teaching Suggestion, p. 262.

Reading
- Have students read **O'gaya** and do Activities D-S, pp. 262–264.

Postreading
- Have students work in small groups to do Activity T, p. 264.
- Cooperative Learning, p. 264
- For additional reading practice, see *Practice and Activity Book*, Activity 20, p. 119.

Ecrivons!

Objectives
Students will learn how to use the appropriate style for different types of writing.

- Motivating Activity, p. 265
- Read and discuss **De bons conseils**, p. 265.
- Activity A (**Prewriting**), Activity B (**Writing**), and Activity C (**Postwriting**), p. 265. See the suggestions to accompany these activities on page 265.

Mise en pratique

Objectives
Students will review and integrate all four skills and cultural information in preparation for the Chapter Test.

- Play the audio recording for Activity 1, p. 266 and check for comprehension.
- Activity 2, p. 266. See For Individual Needs: Slower Pace, p. 266.
- Activity 3, p. 267
- Have students work in pairs to do Activities 4 and 5, p. 267.
- Have students do **Que sais-je?**, p. 268, individually or with a partner.

Assessment
- Chapter Test, *Testing Program*, pp. 221–226
- *Test Generator*, Chapter 10
- Project: **Venez à l'aquarium de Pointe-à-Pitre**, *Annotated Teacher's Edition*, p. 243J
- For alternative assessment options, see the *Alternative Assessment Guide*, pp. 25 and 39.

STANDARDS FOR FOREIGN LANGUAGE LEARNING

Lisons! *Pupil's Edition:* (1.2; 2.1; 3.1) *Annotated Teacher's Edition:* (1.2; 1.3; 3.1; 5.1)
Ecrivons! *Pupil's Edition:* (1.3; 5.2) *Annotated Teacher's Edition:* (1.3)
Mise en pratique *Pupil's Edition:* (1.1; 1.2; 3.1; 4.3) *Annotated Teacher's Edition:* (1.1; 1.3; 3.1)

Teacher's Name _____ Class _____ Date _____

CHAPITRE

Laissez les bons temps rouler!

Beginning the Chapter (pp. 270–275)

Activities in the shaded boxes enhance the basic lesson and are ideal for **block scheduling**.

Lesson Plans

Chapter Opener

- Motivating Activity, p. 270
- Photo Flash! and Focusing on Outcomes, p. 271

Mise en train

Objectives

Students will listen as Simon Laforest, who has just arrived in Louisiana from France, talks with his relatives about their family history and the music and festivals of Louisiana.

- Presentation: **L'arrivée à Lafayette,** p. 273 (Audio CD 11)
- Community Link, p. 272.
- Geography Link and History Link, p. 273
- Read and discuss **Note Culturelle** and Culture Note, p. 274. See the related Teaching Suggestion, p. 274.
- Activities 1–4, p. 274. See For Individual Needs: Auditory Learners, p. 274.
- Replay the recording of Scene 4 of **L'arrivée à Lafayette.** Pause the recording after Anne's remarks and have students try to recall what Simon says. Continue playing the recording after each pause to confirm. Then reverse the procedure, having students supply Anne's remarks.
- Have students work in pairs to adapt the conversation between Anne and Simon in Scene 4 to reflect their own tastes.
- Have students work in groups of three to adapt Scene 5, by imagining Simon is visiting their own area.
- Have students do Activity 5, p. 274, in writing. Have students imagine that they traveled to a place of their choice that was mentioned in an earlier chapter, such as Alsace, Brussels, Morocco, Guadeloupe, or Canada.
- Have students draw the Laforest family tree.
- Activity 1, *Practice and Activity Book,* p. 121
- At this time, you may wish to show *Camille et compagnie, Onzième Épisode : Il faut de tout pour faire un gombo* (Videocassette 4) as an alternative or in addition to the **Mise en train,** or you may choose to show the video episode at the end of the chapter to review new material.
- Teaching suggestions and activities, *Video Guide,* pp. 68–69, 70
- Motivating Activity, p. 275
- Presentation: **Rencontre Culturelle,** p. 275
- Read and discuss Culture Notes and Language Notes, p. 275
- Have students read and discuss the questions in **Qu'en penses-tu?,** p. 275.

Resources

For correlated print and audio-visual materials, *see Annotated Teacher's Edition,* pp. 269A–269B.

STANDARDS FOR FOREIGN LANGUAGE LEARNING

Chapter Opener *Pupil's Edition:* (1.2) *Annotated Teacher's Edition:* (1.1; 1.3; 2.1; 2.2; 3.2; 4.1; 5.1)
Mise en train *Pupil's Edition:* (1.2; 2.1; 4.3) *Annotated Teacher's Edition:* (2.1; 2.2; 5.1; 5.2)

CHAPITRE **11** Laissez les bons temps rouler!

Première étape (pp. 276–279)

Activities in the shaded boxes enhance the basic lesson and are ideal for **block scheduling**.

Lesson Plans

Objectives
Students will learn to ask for confirmation, ask for and give opinions, agree and disagree.

Motivate
Jump Start! and Motivate, p. 276

Teach
1. Presentation: **Comment dit-on… ?**, p. 276
2. Play the audio recording for Activity 6, p. 276 (Audio CD 11) and check for comprehension.
   To extend Activity 6, have students work in small groups to write conversations in which they get reacquainted at their ten-year class reunion.
3. Activities 7 and 8, p. 276
4. Do Presentation: **Vocabulaire** and read and discuss **Note Culturelle**, p. 277. See For Individual Needs: Auditory Learners, p. 277.
   For Individual Needs: Kinesthetic Learners, p. 277
   TPR, p. 277
5. Play the audio recording for Activity 9, p. 277 and check for comprehension.
6. Have students work in groups to do Activities 10–12, pp. 277–278. See Building on Previous Skills, p. 278.
7. Presentation: **Comment dit-on… ?**, p. 278
8. Read and discuss **A la française**, p. 279.
9. Play the audio recording for Activity 13, p. 278 and check for comprehension.
10. Activities 14 and 15, p. 279. See the related Teaching Suggestions, p. 279.
11. Have students do Activities 16 and 17, p. 279, in writing.

Additional Practice Options for Première étape
- *Grammar and Vocabulary Workbook*, pp. 96–97
- *Practice and Activity Book*, pp. 122–125
- Communicative Activities 11-1A and 11-1B, *Activities for Communication*, pp. 41–42
- Situation 11-1: Interview and Role-play, *Activities for Communication*, pp. 109–110
- Realia 11-1, *Activities for Communication*, pp. 81, 83
- Additional Listening Activities 11-1, 11-2 and 11-3, *Listening Activities*, pp. 87–88 (Audio CD 11)
- *Interactive CD-ROM Program* (Disc 3)
- *Teaching Transparency 11-1, Teaching Transparencies*
- Additional Grammar Practice, *Pupil's Edition*, Activity 1, p. R78

Close
Close, p. 279

Assess
Quiz 11-1A, Quiz 11-1B, *Testing Program*, pp. 235–238 and/or Performance Assessment, *Annotated Teacher's Edition*, p. 279

STANDARDS FOR FOREIGN LANGUAGE LEARNING
Première étape *Pupil's Edition*: (1.1; 1.2; 1.3; 2.1; 3.2; 4.1; 4.2; 4.3; 5.2) *Annotated Teacher's Edition*: (1.1; 1.2; 1.3; 2.2; 3.1; 3.2; 4.1; 4.3; 5.1; 5.2)

Teacher's Name _____ Class _____ Date _____

CHAPITRE 11

Laissez les bons temps rouler!

Remise en train (pp. 280–282)

Activities in the shaded boxes enhance the basic lesson and are ideal for **block scheduling**.

Lesson Plans

Objectives
Students will listen as Simon Laforest and his relatives dine and dance at a Cajun festival.

- Motivating Activity, p. 280
- Presentation: **Un festival cajun,** p. 281 (Audio CD 11)
- Teaching Suggestions, p. 281
- To reinforce the functions of asking for permission and making arrangements to meet someone, play the opening scene of **Un festival cajun,** and then replay the opening scene of **Naissance d'une amitié** from Chapter 6, p. 138, in which Raphaël Simenot takes leave of his parents to visit Fez in Morocco. Have students write all the expressions they hear in the two conversations. Then make a list of all the expressions on the board and have students work in pairs to practice them in brief exchanges.
- Replay the second and third scenes of **Un festival cajun** in which Anne suggests what they might do in New Orleans. Begin with Anne's line **Tu sais, si ça te plaît, on pourrait…** and end with … **Oh là là! Tu as vu l'heure?** Then have partners choose the setting of a previous chapter (**Bruxelles, Fès, Montréal, Tunis, la République centrafricaine…**) and recreate this conversation, adapting it to their chosen locale.
- To practice the functions of making recommendations, ordering and asking for detail, replay Scene 4 of **Un festival cajun** in which the family recommends Cajun food to Simon in the restaurant. Then have students role-play a scene in which an American student is explaining the menu at a fast-food restaurant to a foreign-exchange student.
- Activity 19, p. 280
- In Activity 19, after students have reordered the summary sentences correctly, have them rewrite the sentences in the **passé composé,** expanding them with additional phrases or clauses.
- Activities 20 and 21, p. 281
- As a variation of Activity 20, replay the recording of **Un festival cajun** and pause after the expressions that accomplish the functions listed in the activity. Have students listen with books closed and identify the communicative function as you pause after each expression.
- Do Activity 21, p. 281, as a class discussion.
- Activity 9, *Practice and Activity Book,* p. 126
- As an alternative or in addition to the **Remise en train,** you may wish to show *Camille et compagnie, Onzième Épisode : Il faut de tout pour faire un gombo* on Videocassette 4 again. For suggestions and activities, see the *Video Guide,* pp. 68–70.
- Motivating Activity, p. 282
- Do Presentation: **Panorama Culturel,** p. 282, using *Video Program* (Videocassette 4).
- Read and discuss the questions in **Qu'en penses-tu?,** p. 282.
- Suggestions and activities for **Panorama Culturel,** *Video Guide,* pp. 69, 71
- Activity 19, *Practice and Activity Book,* p. 132

STANDARDS FOR FOREIGN LANGUAGE LEARNING
Remise en train *Pupil's Edition:* (1.2; 2.1; 3.1; 4.2) *Annotated Teacher's Edition:* (1.2; 2.1; 2.2)

Allez, viens! Level 3

CHAPITRE 11

Laissez les bons temps rouler!

Deuxième étape (pp. 283–287)

Activities in the shaded boxes enhance the basic lesson and are ideal for **block scheduling**.

Lesson Plans

Objectives
Students will learn to ask for explanations, make observations and give impressions.

Motivate
Jump Start! and Motivate, p. 283

Teach
1. Presentation: **Comment dit-on… ?** and **A la française**, p. 283
2. Play the audio recording for Activity 22, p. 283 and check for comprehension.
3. Activities 23 and 24, pp. 283–284. See Building on Previous Skills, p. 284.
4. Presentation: **Vocabulaire**, p. 284. See Culture Notes, p. 284.
5. Play the audio recording for Activity 25, p. 285 and check for comprehension.
   Use the photos in Activity 25, p. 285, to practice asking for explanations. Have students take turns asking each other and explaining what is pictured.
6. Activity 26, p. 285
7. Have students work in pairs to do Activity 27, p. 285. See the related Teaching Suggestion, p. 285.
   Have students work in small groups to do Activity 28, p. 285.
8. Presentation: **Comment dit-on… ?**, p. 286
9. Play the audio recording for Activity 29, p. 286 and check for comprehension.
10. Review **Tu te rappelles?**, p. 286.
11. Activities 30 and 31, pp. 286–287
12. Game 6, Chapter 11, *Interative CD-ROM Program* (Disc 3)
13. Activity 12, *Grammar and Vocabulary Workbook*, p. 101
    Have students imagine they are visiting one of the places mentioned in an earlier chapter and rewrite the letter in Activity 31, p. 287, accordingly.
14. Activity 32, p. 287. See For Individual Needs: Auditory Learners, p 287.
15. Have students work in pairs to do Activity 33, p. 287.

Additional Practice Options for Deuxième étape
- *Grammar and Vocabulary Workbook,* pp. 98–101
- *Practice and Activity Book,* pp. 127–130
- Communicative Activities 11-2A and 11-2B, *Activities for Communication,* pp. 43–44
- Situations 11-2 and 11-3: Interview and Role-play, *Activities for Communication,* pp. 109–110
- Realia 11-2, *Activities for Communication,* pp. 82–83
- Additional Listening Activities 11-4, 11-5 and 11-6, *Listening Activities,* pp. 88–89 (Audio CD 11)
- *Interactive CD-ROM Program* (Disc 3)
- *Teaching Transparency 11-2, Teaching Transparencies*
- Additional Grammar Practice, *Pupil's Edition,* Activities 2–4, p. R78

Close
Close, p. 287

Assess
Quiz 11-2A, Quiz 11-2B, *Testing Program,* pp. 239–242 and/or Performance Assessment, *Annotated Teacher's Edition,* p. 287

STANDARDS FOR FOREIGN LANGUAGE LEARNING
Deuxième étape *Pupil's Edition:* (1.1; 1.2; 1.3; 2.1; 2.2; 3.1; 3.2; 4.1; 4.3) *Annotated Teacher's Edition:* (1.1; 1.2; 1.3; 2.1; 2.2; 3.1; 4.1; 4.2; 5.1; 5.2)

CHAPITRE 11

Laissez les bons temps rouler!

Ending the Chapter (pp. 288–295)

Activities in the shaded boxes enhance the basic lesson and are ideal for **block scheduling**.

CHAPITRE 11

Lesson Plans

Lisons!

Objectives
Students will learn to understand a dialect.

Prereading
- Motivating Activity, p. 288
- Read and discuss **De bons conseils**, p. 288.
- Activity A, p. 288. See the related Teaching Suggestion, p. 288.

Reading
- Have students read **Froumi et Grasshopper** and do Activities B–E, pp. 288–289. See Language-to-Language/Music Link, p. 289.
- Have students read **La Cigale et la fourmi** on page 290 and do Activities F–I, pp. 289–290.
- Activities J–K, p. 290

Postreading
- Activity L, p. 290. See the Teaching Suggestion and For Individual Needs: Challenge, p. 290.
- For additional reading practice, see *Practice and Activity Book*, Activity 18, p. 131.

Ecrivons!

Objectives
Students will learn how to use poetic devices.

- Motivating Activity, p. 291
- Read and discuss **De bons conseils**, p. 291.
- Activity A (**Prewriting**), Activity B (**Writing**) and Activity C (**Postwriting**), p. 291. See the suggestions to accompany these activities on page 291.

Mise en pratique

Objectives
Students will review and integrate all four skills and cultural information in preparation for the Chapter Test.

- Activity 1, p. 292. See the related Teaching Suggestions, p. 292.
- Play the audio recording for Activity 2, p. 293 and check for comprehension.
- Have students work in pairs or small groups to do Activities 3–5, p. 293.
- Have students do **Que sais-je?**, p. 294, individually or with a partner.

Assessment
- Chapter Test, *Testing Program*, pp. 243–248
- *Test Generator*, Chapter 11
- **Jeu de rôle**, *Pupil's Edition*, p. 293 or Situation Cards, *Activities for Communication*, pp. 109–110
- Project: **La cuisine cajun**, *Annotated Teacher's Edition*, p. 269J
- For alternative assessment options, see the *Alternative Assessment Guide*, pp. 26 and 40.

STANDARDS FOR FOREIGN LANGUAGE LEARNING

Lisons! *Pupil's Edition:* (1.2; 2.1; 3.1; 3.2; 4.1; 4.2; 4.3) *Annotated Teacher's Edition:* (5.2)
Ecrivons! *Pupil's Edition:* (1.3; 5.2) *Annotated Teacher's Edition:* (1.3)
Mise en pratique *Pupil's Edition:* (1.1; 1.2; 1.3; 2.1; 2.2; 3.1; 4.3; 5.2) *Annotated Teacher's Edition:* (1.1; 2.2; 3.1; 4.3)

CHAPITRE 12 · Echanges sportifs et culturels

Beginning the Chapter (pp. 296–300)

Activities in the shaded boxes enhance the basic lesson and are ideal for **block scheduling**.

Lesson Plans

Chapter Opener

- Motivating Activity, p. 296
- Photo Flash!, p. 296
- Focusing on Outcomes and Teaching Suggestions, p. 297

Mise en train

Objectives

Students will listen as four young athletes discuss their preparations for the Olympic Games.

- Motivating Activity, p. 298
- Before you play each scene as recommended in the Presentation, have students read the questions in Activity 1, p. 300. Then ask them to listen carefully to discover not only how each athlete feels, but also how the person who is speaking with the athlete feels. Is the person encouraging, apprehensive or non-supportive? Does the person offer advice?
- Presentation: **A nous les Jeux olympiques,** p. 299 (Audio CD 12)
- In Scene 3, Marie-José Pérec is mentioned. She is a champion track star born in Guadeloupe. You might have students read or reread Realia 10-1, *Activities for Communication*, p. 78, which gives information about Marie-José Pérec.
- Teaching Suggestion, p. 299
- For Individual Needs: Auditory Learners, p. 299
- Read and discuss **Note Culturelle** and Culture Notes, p. 300.
- Activities 1–4, p. 300
- In Activity 4, have students find one expression for each function and then compare their findings in small groups.
- Have students do Activity 5, p. 300, in writing. In Activity 5, students might relate their participation in theater, chorus, or in an academic competition rather than in a sporting event.
- Activity 1, *Practice and Activity Book,* p. 133
- At this time, you may wish to show **Camille et compagnie,** *Douzième Épisode : Une sauterelle pleine d'avenir* (Videocassette 4) as an alternative or in addition to the **Mise en train,** or you may choose to show the video episode at the end of the chapter to review new material.
- Teaching suggestions and activities, *Video Guide,* pp. 74 and 76

Resources

For correlated print and audio-visual materials, see *Annotated Teacher's Edition,* pp. 295A–295B.

CHAPITRE 12

STANDARDS FOR FOREIGN LANGUAGE LEARNING

Chapter Opener *Pupil's Edition:* (1.2) *Annotated Teacher's Edition:* (1.3; 3.1; 5.2)
Mise en train *Pupil's Edition:* (1.2) *Annotated Teacher's Edition:* (1.2; 3.1)

Teacher's Name _____ Class _____ Date _____

CHAPITRE 12
Echanges sportifs et culturels
Première étape (pp. 301–305)

Activities in the shaded boxes enhance the basic lesson and are ideal for **block scheduling**.

Lesson Plans

Objectives
Students will learn to express anticipation, make suppositions and express certainty and doubt.

Motivate
Jump Start! and Motivate, p. 301

Teach
1. Presentation: **Vocabulaire**, p. 301
2. Teaching Suggestion and TPR, p. 301
3. Play the audio recording for Activity 6, p. 301 (Audio CD 12) and check for comprehension.
4. Activities 7 and 8, p. 302. See the related Teaching Suggestions and For Individual Needs: Slower Pace, p. 302.
   Group Work, p. 302
5. Review **Tu te rappelles?** and the expressions for giving advice in Chapter 5, p. 124 and then have students do Activity 9, p. 303.
6. Conduct the poll suggested in Activity 10, p. 303. See the related Teaching Suggestion, p. 303.
   Have students do Activity 11, p. 303, in writing.
7. Presentation: **Comment dit-on... ?**, p. 304.
8. Play the audio recording for Activity 12, p. 304 and check for comprehension.
9. Game 2, Chapter 12, *Interactive CD-ROM Program* (Disc 3)
10. Activity 9, *Practice and Activity Book*, p. 137
11. Presentation: **Grammaire**, p. 304.
12. Activities 6 and 7, *Grammar and Vocabulary Workbook*, p. 104
13. Activities 13 and 14, p. 305
    Game: **Quand je...**, p. 304
14. Have students work in pairs to do Activity 15, p. 305.
15. Have students do Activity 16, p. 305, in writing.

Additional Practice Options for Première étape
- *Grammar and Vocabulary Workbook*, pp. 102–104
- *Practice and Activity Book*, pp. 134–137
- Communicative Activities 12-1A and 12-1B, *Activities for Communication*, pp. 45–46
- Situation 12-1: Interview and Role-play, *Activities for Communication*, pp. 111–112
- Realia 12-1, *Activities for Communication*, pp. 84, 86
- Additional Listening Activities 12-1, 12-2 and 12-3, *Listening Activities*, pp. 95–96 (Audio CD 12)
- *Interactive CD-ROM Program* (Disc 3)
- *Teaching Transparency 12-1, Teaching Transparencies*
- Additional Grammar Practice, *Pupil's Edition*, Activities 1–3, p. R79

Close
Close, p. 305

Assess
Quiz 12-1A, Quiz 12-1B, *Testing Program*, pp. 257–260 and/or Performance Assessment, *Annotated Teacher's Edition*, p. 305

STANDARDS FOR FOREIGN LANGUAGE LEARNING
Première étape *Pupil's Edition:* (1.1; 1.2; 1.3; 4.1; 5.2) *Annotated Teacher's Edition:* (1.1; 1.2; 1.3; 2.2; 3.1; 5.2)

58 Lesson Planner

Allez, viens! Level 3

Copyright © by Holt, Rinehart and Winston. All rights reserved.

CHAPITRE 12

CHAPITRE

12

Echanges sportifs et culturels

Remise en train (pp. 306–307)

Activities in the shaded boxes enhance the basic lesson and are ideal for **block scheduling.**

Lesson Plans

Objectives

Students will listen as athletes talk about their countries, make arrangements to visit each other, and congratulate or console each other on their performances as they watch the basketball finals at the Olympics.

- Motivating Activity, p. 306
- Presentation: **Un rendez-vous sportif et cuturel**, p. 307 (Audio CD 12)
- Before playing Scenes 1 and 2, tell students to listen carefully to discover the blunder Yvonne makes. Before playing Scenes 3 and 4, ask students to listen carefully to discover why Hélène is sad and what Onélia suggests to cheer her up. Likewise, ask students to listen carefully to Scene 5 to learn how Julie and Jean-Paul fared in their events at the Olympics.
- Have students work in pairs to select a country they are unfamiliar with and write down whatever preconceived impressions they might have of that country. Then have them do research to confirm or correct these impressions. Finally, partners should use the information to create a conversation in French, modeled on the one between Mademba and Yvonne in **Un rendez-vous sportif et culturel,** in which one partner pretends to be a native of that country and corrects the false impressions of the other.
- Replay the conversation between Hélène and Ophélia. Have partners imagine they are from two other countries and recreate the conversation, making any necessary changes.
- Activities 17–20, pp. 306–307
- In Activity 20, have students also find expressions for consoling **(Ne t'en fais pas! Ça peut arriver à tout le monde!)** and for asking for and giving opinions **(Je trouve ça dommage que les gens ne s'intéressent pas à la culture des autres. A ton avis, qui va gagner?).**
- Have students work in pairs to do the Teaching Suggestions related to Activity 20, p. 307.
- Have students work in small groups to do Activity 21, p. 307. Then have volunteers from each group share their information with the rest of the class. If students have not met anyone from another country, they might talk about someone they've met from another state or region of their own country.
- Activity 10, *Practice and Activity Book,* p. 138
- As an alternative or in addition to the **Remise en train,** you may wish to show *Camille et compagnie, Douzième Épisode : Une sauterelle pleine d'avenir* on Videocassette 4 again. For suggestions and activities, see the *Video Guide,* pp. 74 and 76.

STANDARDS FOR FOREIGN LANGUAGE LEARNING

Remise en train *Pupil's Edition:* (1.1; 1.2) *Annotated Teacher's Edition:* (1.1; 1.2)

CHAPITRE 12

Echanges sportifs et culturels

Deuxième étape (pp. 308–311)

Activities in the shaded boxes enhance the basic lesson and are ideal for **block scheduling.**

Lesson Plans

C H A P I T R E 12

Objectives
Students will learn to inquire and to express excitement and disappointment.

Motivate
Jump Start! and Motivate, p. 308

Teach
1. Presentation: **Vocabulaire,** p, 308. See Additional Practice and Geography Link, p. 308.
2. Go over **Tu te rappelles,** p. 308 and then have students do Activities 22 and 23, pp. 308–309.
   To extend Activity 23, have students do research on a city of their choice and then recommend that city to a partner.
3. Presentation: **Comment dit-on... ?,** p. 309. See the related Teaching Suggestion, p. 309.
4. Play the audio recording for Activity 24, p. 309 and check for comprehension.
5. Have students work in pairs to do Activity 25, p. 309.
   To extend Activity 25, have students continue the completed conversation on their own.
6. Have students do Activity 26, p. 309, in writing.
7. Do Motivating Activity and Presentation: **Panorama Culturel,** p. 310, using *Video Program* (Videocassette 4).
   Suggestions and activities for **Panorama Culturel,** *Video Guide,* pp. 75 and 77
   Activity 18, *Practice and Activity Book,* p. 144
8. Have students work in pairs to do Activity 27, p. 311.
9. Presentation: **Comment dit-on... ?,** p. 311
10. Play the audio recording for Activity 28, p. 311 and check for comprehension.
11. Activities 29 and 30, p. 311. See For Individual Needs: Slower Pace, p. 311.
12. To extend Activity 30, have students exchange postcards and write each other a reply.
13. Have students work in groups to do Activity 31, p. 311.

Additional Practice Options for Deuxième étape
- *Grammar and Vocabulary Workbook,* pp. 105–107
- *Practice and Activity Book,* pp. 139–142
- Communicative Activities 12-2A and 12-2B, *Activities for Communication,* pp. 47–48
- Situations 12-2 and 12-3: Interview and Role-play, *Activities for Communication,* pp. 111–112
- Realia 12-2, *Activities for Communication,* pp. 85–86
- Additional Listening Activities 12-4, 12-5 and 12-6, *Listening Activities,* pp. 96–97 (Audio CD 12)
- *Interactive CD-ROM Program* (Disc 3)
- *Teaching Transparency 12-2, Teaching Transparencies*
- Additional Grammar Practice, *Pupil's Edition,* Activities 4–5, p. R80

Close
Close, p. 311

Assess
Quiz 12-2A, Quiz 12-2B, *Testing Program,* pp. 261–264 and/or Performance Assessment, *Annotated Teacher's Edition,* p. 311

STANDARDS FOR FOREIGN LANGUAGE LEARNING
Deuxième étape *Pupil's Edition:* (1.1; 1.2; 1.3; 2.1; 2.2; 3.1; 4.2; 5.2) *Annotated Teacher's Edition:* (1.1; 1.2; 1.3; 2.1; 3.1; 4.2)

Echanges sportifs et culturels

C H A P I T R E

12

Ending the Chapter (pp. 312–319)

Activities in the shaded boxes enhance the basic lesson and are ideal for **block scheduling**.

Lesson Plans

Lisons!

Objectives
Students will learn to combine reading strategies.

Prereading
- Motivating Activity, p. 312
- Read and discuss **De bons conseils**, p. 312.
- Activities A and B, p. 312. See Motivating Activity, p. 312.

Reading
- Have students read **Le sport et le monde francophone**, pp. 312–313 and do Activities C–F, pp. 312–313.
- Have students read **World Cup 1998: Allez les bleus!** and do Activities G–J, p. 314.
- See Teaching Suggestions, p. 313.

Postreading
- Activity K, p. 314
- See Teaching Suggestion, p. 314.
- For additional reading practice, see *Practice and Activity Book*, Activity 17, p. 143.

Ecrivons!

Objectives
Students will learn about doing research.

- Motivating Activity, p. 315. Read and discuss **De bons conseils**, p. 315.
- Activity A **(Prewriting)**, Activity B **(Writing)** and Activity C **(Postwriting)**, p. 315. See the suggestions to accompany these activities on page 315.

Mise en pratique

Objectives
Students will review and integrate all four skills and cultural information in preparation for the Chapter Test.

- Activity 1, p. 316. See Career Path, p. 316.
- Play the audio recording for Activity 2, p. 317 and check for comprehension.
- Activities 3–5, p. 317
- Have students do **Que sais-je?**, p. 318, individually or with a partner.

Assessment
- Chapter Test, *Testing Program*, pp. 265–270
- *Test Generator*, Chapter 12
- Situation Cards, *Activities for Communication*, pp. 111–112
- Project: **Cette année-là aux Jeux olympiques**, *Annotated Teacher's Edition*, p. 295J
- For alternative assessment options, see the *Alternative Assessment Guide*, pp. 27 and 41.

STANDARDS FOR FOREIGN LANGUAGE LEARNING
Lisons! *Pupil's Edition:* (1.2; 2.1; 3.1; 3.2; 4.1) *Annotated Teacher's Edition:* (1.2; 1.3; 2.2; 3.1; 3.2)
Ecrivons! *Pupil's Edition:* (1.3; 3.2; 5.2) *Annotated Teacher's Edition:* (1.3)
Mise en pratique *Pupil's Edition:* (1.1; 1.2; 1.3; 3.1; 3.2) *Annotated Teacher's Edition:* (1.1; 2.1; 3.1; 4.3)

C H A P I T R E   1 2

Allez, viens! Level 3